LIGHT A FIRE AND WATCH IT BURN

QUALITATIVE RESEARCH METHODOLOGIES: TRADITIONS, DESIGNS, AND PEDAGOGIES

EDITED BY KATHLEEN DEMARRAIS, MELISSA FREEMAN, JORI HALL, AND KATHRYN ROULSTON

The *Qualitative Research Methodologies: Traditions, Designs, and Pedagogies* series is designed to encourage qualitative researchers to look both backward and forward in the field of qualitative inquiry. We invite authors to submit proposals for both single-authored books and edited volumes focused on particular qualitative designs situated within their historical, theoretical, and disciplinary/cross-disciplinary contexts. Pieces might include a tradition's or design's historical roots and key scholars, ways the approach has changed over time, as well as ethical and methodological considerations in the use of that particular research approach. They may also provide an introduction to contemporary designs created at the intersection of multiple, theoretical, and often assumed incommensurable historical paths. In addition, we encourage authors to submit proposals for books focused on the pedagogy of qualitative research methodologies that interrogate how we prepare researchers new to qualitative research methodologies with the theoretical, methodological, and ethical understandings and skills for their work.

Those interested in being considered for inclusion in the series should send a prospectus (https://zfrmz.com/rmlvGq7xgL2RTgPkByk9), CV, and cover letter to: Kathleen deMarrais (kathleen@uga.edu).

Books in the Series:

Focus Groups: Culturally Responsive Approaches for Qualitative Inquiry and Program Evaluation
by Jori N. Hall (2020)

Exploring the Archives: A Beginner's Guide for Qualitative Researchers
by Kathryn Roulston and Kathleen deMarrais (2021)

Transformative Autoethnography for Practitioners: Change Processes and Practices for Individuals and Groups
by Kathy-Ann C. Hernandez, Wendy Bilgen, and Heewon Chang (2022)

Quests for Questioners: Inventive Approaches to Qualitative Interviews
edited by Kathryn Roulston (2023)

The Action Research Dissertation: Learning from Leading Change
by Karen E. Watkins, Erica Gilbertson, and Aliki Nicolaides (2023)

Qualitative Research Design and Methods: An Introduction
by Kathleen deMarrais, Kathryn Roulston, and Janie Copple (2024)

Light a Fire and Watch It Burn: Disruptive Qualitative Methods in Education Research
edited by Michael L. Boucher Jr. (2025)

ADVANCE PRAISE FOR

LIGHT A FIRE AND WATCH IT BURN: DISRUPTIVE QUALITATIVE METHODS IN EDUCATION RESEARCH

"*Light a Fire and Watch it Burn* highlights the power of education scholars to rupture the established boundaries of qualitative research. From decolonial approaches to critical analyses to creative inquiries, this collection illustrates ways we can understand the world anew."

Wayne Au,
Dean and Professor,
University of Washington
Bothell School of Educational Studies

"Michael Boucher's *Light a Fire and Watch It Burn: Disruptive Qualitative Methods in Education Research* un-does and re-does qualitative methods and education to bring urgency back to educational experiences of students, teachers, community members, professors. This fresh new take on qualitative methods takes up the best and most urgent tradition in educational research with a focus on Freirean, up-from-below, emancipation. Purchase it, use it, teach it –."

Jim Jupp,
Professor and Chair of the Department of Teaching and Learning,
University of Texas Rio Grande Valley

"Each chapter strikes a match and lets it fall into dry, waiting fields—a spark of inquiry that refuses to be caged by the brittle fences of traditional research and storytelling. No findings are embalmed here in lifeless prose; instead, each page stretches across new territories of thought, where education lives not as a system, but as a contained blaze.

Within these pages, readers will find not only the careful bones of methodology and theory, but the crackling energy of disruption: a call to dismantle systems of oppression, and to empower those too long silenced to step boldly into the light."

Peter McLaren,
Professor Emeritus,
University of California Los Angeles

"*Light a Fire and Watch It Burn: Disruptive Qualitative Methods in Education Research* boldly challenges traditional qualitative inquiry by centering marginalized epistemologies and transformative methodologies. Building on and complimenting foundational texts in educational research, this volume introduces practice-oriented approaches that reject prescriptive norms and embrace social justice-driven research. Through powerful narratives, it explores how qualitative methods can ignite change, work towards dismantling systems of power, and amplify silenced and marginalized voices. Featuring contributions from both seasoned scholars and emerging voices, this book is a call to action: to reimagine research not just as inquiry, but as resistance, revolution, and renewal"

Robert J. Helfenbein, PhD,
Professor of Curriculum Studies,
Mercer University

LIGHT A FIRE AND WATCH IT BURN

Disruptive Qualitative Methods in Education Research

EDITED BY MICHAEL L. BOUCHER, JR.

Myers Education Press
Gorham, Maine

Myers Education Press

Copyright © 2025 | Myers Education Press, LLC
Published by Myers Education Press, LLC
P.O. Box 424
Gorham, ME 04038

Myers Education Press is an academic publisher specializing in books, e-books, and digital content in the field of education. All of our books are subjected to a rigorous peer review process and produced in compliance with the standards of the Council on Library and Information Resources.

Library of Congress Cataloging-in-Publication Data available from Library of Congress.

13-digit ISBN 978-1-9755-0719-0 (paperback)
13-digit ISBN 978-1-9755-0721-3 (library networkable e-edition)
13-digit ISBN 978-1-9755-0721-3 (consumer e-edition)

Printed in the United States of America.

All first editions printed on acid-free paper that meets the American National Standards Institute Z39-48 standard.

Books published by Myers Education Press may be purchased at special quantity discount rates for groups, workshops, training organizations, and classroom usage. Please call our customer service department at 1-800-232-0223 for details.

Cover design by .

Visit us on the web at **www.myersedpress.com** to browse our complete list of titles.

Dedication

To my students—past, present, and future—whose questions, courage, and determination inspire me to keep learning, growing, and seeking new ways to teach and learn, your voices have shaped the need for this work, and your brilliance fuels its purpose.

To the scholars whose groundbreaking work has illuminated my path and enriched my understanding, your insights have transformed my research and informed my teaching, reminding me of the power of people's experiences to disrupt, empower, and uplift.

To Dr. Robert Helfenbein—my mentor, friend, and model of community-engaged scholarship. When I was unsure where to turn, he introduced me to the methodological texts I needed to light fires and disrupt the comfortable. This book is a testament to his generosity, guidance, and profound influence.

And to my wife, Karen—my steadfast partner, greatest encourager, and constant source of inspiration—your support and love remind me what is most important every day.

Michael L. Boucher, Jr.

Contents

Acknowledgments

THIS BOOK WOULD NOT HAVE been possible without the invaluable contributions of Ms. Amy Castillo, whose dedication and insight enriched every aspect of this project. Amy is an accomplished teacher, education leader, and academic coordinator, currently pursuing her second master's degree in Curriculum and Instruction at Texas A&M University-San Antonio.

As a master's student, Amy exemplifies what it means to be a scholar and a learner. Her research reflects a dedication to examining complex and personal topics and underscores how disruptive qualitative methods can amplify the wisdom of marginalized people. Thank you, Amy, for your unwavering commitment to this work, invaluable feedback, and contributions. It has been an honor to work alongside you on this journey.

Series Foreword

Melissa Freeman and Kathryn Roulston

DEAR READER, ARE YOU READY to jump into the flames of change ignited by the authors of this edited collection? Regardless of whether you believe these flames are engulfing what surrounds them, quietly smoldering below the surface, or fueling acts of renewal and rebirth, playing with fire carries risk. Fire stands apart from other common elements—air, water, earth—because it is not a substance or gas but a chemical reaction when the conditions are right. "Fire is a shape-shifter, taking its character from its context" (Pyne, 2016, p. 6). Fire is ignition, combustion, illumination, destroyer of life while also being necessary to life. As we have seen in the terrible fires that have afflicted communities across a planet encompassed by climate change, fire can leap boundaries, propelled by forces beyond human control. Both awe-inspiring and devastating, fire represents an amazing tool for heating, cooking, illuminating, and bringing communities together, all while behaving in spectacularly unexpected ways, causing both devastating destructions, and providing pyrophilic plants the means to reproduce.

These chapters attempt to leap boundaries, just as fire does. As you engage with the pages of this edited collection, we hope you will be challenged to think about your own research differently, to consider incorporating some methods that you have not yet used, and to think deeply about what it means to "disrupt" research. Ta-Nehisi Coates (2024), in his book *The Message*, writes:

> We require another standard—one that sees the sharpening of our writing as the sharpening of our quality of light. And with that light we are charged with examining the stories we have been told, and how they undergird the politics we have accepted, and then telling new stories ourselves. (p. 19)

This volume provides ideas for how qualitative researchers in education might tell new stories about our world. Some of you will have already committed to doing research that opposes the systems of oppression that Coates writes about. You have engaged in research against the grain that others have questioned. You have encountered audience members who ask you: "What's the point?"; "How are your findings valid?" For these readers, this volume will introduce you to a group of scholars with whom you might align your work—scholars to whom you might reach out with invitations to build community. And if you have yet to "disrupt" your approaches to understanding the world, read on. . . .

The verb *disrupt* derives from the Latin *disruptus*, meaning to "break apart, burst, shatter, separate forcibly; *esp*. interrupt the normal continuity of (an activity etc.); throw into disorder" (Brown, 1993, Vol. 1, p. 702). Collectively, the authors in this volume aim to disrupt the routine ways in which education scholars across the world think about and conduct qualitative inquiry. Following in the spirit of other edited texts in education research advocating for critical approaches (see for example Brown et al., 2014; Matias, 2021; Paris & Winn, 2014; Winkle-Wagner et al., 2019; Young & Diem, 2024, to name a sampling), the authors in this collection further methodological approaches that challenge the claim to neutrality, objectivity, and dispassion commonly promoted in research texts. To do this, they carry out culturally sustaining, decolonizing, and participatory approaches, narrative inquiry and community storytelling, and sonic and arts-based methodologies, while drawing on theoretical frameworks such as Indigenous epistemologies and concepts, Black feminist thought, decolonial, anti-colonial, and posthumanist theories, critical theories of whiteness, and liberation theology. They also use concepts from scholars such as bell hooks, Paolo Freire, Patti Lather, William Pinar, and Norman Denzin, all of whom have long challenged the status quo in terms of how qualitative inquiry is thought to work by those who have not studied the wide variety of approaches available.

When teaching qualitative methods, we often tell students to begin with what they know, whether this knowledge is gained from personal or professional experience or derived from disciplinary training. What stands out in this collection of reflective essays on research practice is that each author develops a methodological approach that rekindles a core facet of their being in ways that challenge the compartmentalization and boundaries distinguishing "valid" research from research considered too subjective, biased, or personal. Working from a distinct place of knowing, the authors collectively restore connection to spirit, embodied sense, community, solidarity, and care. In diverse and unique ways, the authors break epistemological barriers, blurring assumed theory and practice divides. Yet, they are united in their commitments to change and the development of ethical relationships with the participants with whom they work. They seek to develop culturally appropriate and relevant approaches to research that center marginalized voices and illuminate subjugated knowledges.

This volume generously introduces readers to a wide variety of methods that new and veteran education scholars can use to disrupt their thinking about what they know about the world. And yes, perhaps this will entail lighting fires, and watching prior thinking and ways of knowing become enveloped by the flames of alternative approaches. Each chapter provides a welcoming introduction to a research approach, before showing how it might be applied by others, and providing examples of studies that demonstrate their disruptive potential. Developing each method in an organic way, the authors show how flames can leap boundaries and ignite unexpected things. Zachary Casey's final chapter provides a word of caution to all researchers: Methods are tools that can be used in both anti-oppressive and oppressive ways. The challenge, then, for all qualitative researchers to is take up and use the tools suggested in this volume in ethical ways that help us to not only understand the world, but to provide ways for participants themselves to make the changes that enable them to live full and rich lives that support and sustain growth and life on this planet we call earth.

References

Brown, L. (Ed.). (1993). *The new shorter Oxford English dictionary* (Vol. 1). Clarendon Press.

Brown, R. N., Carducci, R., & Kuby, C. R. (Eds.). (2014). *Disrupting qualitative inquiry: Possibilities and tensions in educational research.* Peter Lang.

Coates, T-N. (2024). *The message.* One World.

Matias, C. E. (Ed.) (2021). *The handbook of critical theoretical research methods in education.* Routledge.

Paris, D., & Winn, M. T. (Eds.). (2014). *Humanizing research: Decolonizing qualitative inquiry with youth and communities.* Sage.

Pyne, S. J. (2016). Fire in the mind: Changing understandings of fire in Western civilization. *Philosophical Transactions of the Royal Society B*, 371(1696), 20150166. https://royalsocietypublishing.org/doi/full/10.1098/rstb.2015.0166

Winkle-Wagner, R., Lee-Johnson, J., & Gaskew, A. N. (Eds.). (2019). *Critical theory and qualitative data analysis in education.* Routledge.

Young, M. D., & Diem, S. (Eds.). (2024). *Handbook of critical education research: Qualitative, quantitative, and emerging approaches.* Routledge.

INTRODUCTION

Why does qualitative research need to be disruptive and disrupted?

Amy Castillo and Michael L. Boucher, Jr.

QUALITATIVE RESEARCH HAS BECOME A cornerstone of education inquiry, providing tools to understand complex human experiences. Foundational texts such as those by Creswell and Poth (2016), Mertler (2021), Patton (2014), and Ravitch and Carl (2019) offer comprehensive guidance for students and researchers. These works lay the groundwork for understanding qualitative methods, including participant selection, observation, interviewing, coding, analysis, and the mechanics of creating research proposals and dissertations. As educators and researchers, we owe much of our professional growth to these foundational texts, which professors rely on to teach master's and doctoral students.

However, as I (Amy) engaged with diverse scholarly communities and explored emerging literature, I encountered qualitative methods that challenged traditional methods and models. These often centered marginalized epistemologies, disrupted entrenched systems of oppression, and fostered transformative possibilities for participants and researchers. Unfortunately, these approaches are rarely included in introductory qualitative research texts and are often introduced to researchers only after their formal education, at conferences, or through self-directed exploration.

As a master's student working with my advisor, the gap surrounding these qualitative methods became apparent as I began thinking about my thesis. My chosen topic, *resiliency in Spanish-speaking Latinos after linguistic oppression*, is personal to me, as it reflects the experiences my mother faced as a Spanish-speaking Latina who faced linguistic oppression as a student in the 1960s. The linguistic oppression she encountered led my mother to make the difficult decision not to teach my siblings and me Spanish, fearing we would endure the same oppression she faced as a student.

Reflecting on this personal connection, I realized how traditional research methodologies often fail to capture the subtleties of the lived experiences of oppressed people or provide the tools necessary to explore them authentically. As I researched the topic of linguistic oppression, I discovered my mother was not the only parent who made the same choice for their children. As I have progressed through my master's program, I have become determined to study the lived experiences of Latinos through qualitative research with testimonio as my methodological approach. My goal is to close the gap, contribute to the research, and provide Latinx people with more support and tools to develop resiliency after linguistic oppression.

It is this space that *Light a Fire and Watch It Burn: Disruptive Qualitative Methods in Education Research* seeks to fill. The title encapsulates the essence of the work: qualitative research as a tool to ignite change. The metaphor of *lighting a fire* speaks to the catalytic potential of these methods to spark new ways of thinking, dismantle oppressive structures, and fuel transformative social action. The second part, *watch it burn*, underscores the boldness of these approaches—embracing discomfort in methodology, challenging traditional norms in methods, and encouraging researchers to move beyond the safety of established procedures. It is a challenge to stand close to the conflagration and observe as the fire sparked by questioning and scrutiny engulfs the ontological fuel within the phenomenon under examination. Especially now, as education as a concept is under attack from all sides, education research must reflect the power and urgency of disruptive qualitative methods to revolt against colonial storytelling, subvert dominating ideologies, refuse prescriptive discourse and respectability politics, disrupt canonical conventions, and demand more equitable, inclusive practices (Higginbotham, 1994).

In many ways, qualitative research has always held the potential to be revolutionary. It allows us to center human experience, uncover hidden truths, and amplify marginalized voices. Yet, much of the traditional guidance focuses on the *how-to* or the technical steps necessary to design, conduct, and analyze research. This is, of course, vital. But what if we reimagine qualitative research as a tool for justice? What if we actively seek to disrupt entrenched systems of power and privilege through our methods?

This book complements traditional texts by offering concise, practice-oriented chapters introducing disruptive approaches to knowledge production. Each of the chapters, some written by established scholars and others by newly minted PhDs who have struggled against structures seeking to contain their fire, follow a consistent structure to ensure ease of integration into methods courses:

1. **Technique Overview:** Authors explain the method, citing foundational works and publications illustrating its application.
2. **Disruptive Potential:** Authors discuss how the method challenges systemic oppression and empowers participants.
3. **Theoretical Foundations:** Authors explore the origins and key theorists who shaped the method.
4. **Further Reading and References:** Each chapter includes curated resources for students seeking deeper exploration.
5. **Discussion Questions:** Each chapter includes questions designed to provoke critical thinking and meaningful dialogue among students and instructors. These questions are intended to serve multiple purposes in research methods courses for master's and doctoral students. Their purpose is to deepen understanding of methods and methodologies, examine the potential for disruption, foster reflexivity, connect theory to practice, encourage collaborative dialogue, and prepare for future research.

With 15 chapters, this book is a companion for qualitative research courses, offering instructors the flexibility to integrate individual chapters into weekly lessons. Beyond its use in classrooms, the book is a resource for scholars seeking to expand their methodological repertoire and engage with innovative, equity-centered research practices.

Chapters cover diverse techniques and highlight how these methods can dismantle traditional academic norms and foster more inclusive, participant-centered research. Bias toward quantitative, *data-driven* schooling practices, political pressures, social pressures, and systemic gravitation toward non-controversial topics of inquiry make the pursuit of antiracist and anti-oppressive knowledge even more critical as we struggle through the 21st century. *Light a Fire and Watch It Burn* inspires students and scholars to envision qualitative research as a transformative, justice-oriented struggle. The book is an invitation to embrace the full potential of qualitative inquiry—to ignite curiosity, confront power, and fuel movements for change. By integrating these methods into the fabric of qualitative research education, we can prepare the next generation of scholars to create knowledge that genuinely reflects the diversity of human experience and demands a world where people are brought from the margins, joining together to create learning and meaning.

Below is a summary of each chapter

Brandehoff—Ōiwi methodologies

To honor the moʻōlelo, kūpana, āina of Hawaiʻi and progress her Hānai Pedagogical framework, Brandehoff discusses how she uses ōiwi and "mixed-plate" methodologies in her research. The idea of "mixed-plate" comes from the "rich and diverse background of Native Hawaiians, Japanese, Chinese, Portuguese, Spanish, and other immigrants" who live in Hawaiʻi. These qualitative methodologies involve "talk stories," where individuals from a community share their "personal experiences" with others. Brandehoff also describes the importance of community engagement in building trust and collaborating with community members. Her Hānai Pedagogy framework also emphasizes mentorship and a sense of ʻohana (family).

Jordan—Anticolonial Ethics

Jordan argues that traditional Institutional Review Boards and prevalent methodologies perpetuate colonial ideologies rooted in colonial power structures. Jordan describes an anticolonial ethical praxis based on a four-principled approach, which includes our thinking (theorizing), acting (methodology), reflecting (reflexivity), and relating (answerability).

Patrón-Vargas and Monreal—Rasquache

Patrón-Vargas and Monreal discuss the application of the rasquache methodology as a research approach grounded in Chicanx/Latinx culture. The researchers define rasquache as a resourceful way of creating something out of nothing and being born out of necessity. This methodology can be viewed as a means to disturb the Eurocentric research norms and bring marginalized communities' experiences and ideas to the center.

Samuels—Ethnodrama

This chapter describes ethnodrama, an arts-based research method that integrates ethnography and drama to create a play script derived from qualitative data. The method aims to investigate and portray aspects of the human condition through performance. It requires interviews and other data to create a play script, including participant representation and ethical considerations. This method prioritizes participants' ethical representation and collaboration, using their lived experiences to create socially conscious and artistically meaningful scripts that can challenge dominant narratives and foster understanding.

Gershon and Wozolek—Sonic Methods and Methodology

Gershon and Wozolek critique the dominance of ocular-centric methods in qualitative research, arguing that this focus on sight perpetuates colonial and extractive practices while neglecting the ethical, relational, and justice-oriented potential of sonic methodologies. It emphasizes that listening—both metaphorical and literal—is a central yet undervalued practice in qualitative research and education, fostering deeper connections with research collaborators and challenging traditional power dynamics. Drawing on historical and contemporary scholarship, the authors advocate for a paradigm shift toward sonic attentiveness to enrich educational research and amplify marginalized voices.

Steyn—Currere

Steyn explains how the use of *currere*, which in Latin means *to run the course*, provides a way for educators to utilize their own lived experiences to reflect on and reframe their pedagogical practices. Steyn uses her experiences as a white teacher in South Africa to demonstrate how currere helped her develop culturally responsive and inclusive pedagogy.

Winfield et al.—Duoethnography

Duoethnography is a process where sister scholars share similar experiences, co-create knowledge, challenge power structures, and advocate for social change, as the researchers define. It is a collaborative research method Black and Brown women scholars use to disrupt traditional academic norms. The researchers' goal in using duoethnography is to generate more inclusive and equitable academic discourse.

Monreal—Photovoice

Monreal describes how visual imagery (photo) and narrative (voice) bring together a participatory research method known as *photovoice*. He explains how photovoice empowers marginalized communities by documenting members' lived experiences, raising a critical consciousness through dialogue, and influencing policy change. Photovoice is a powerful tool for battling systems of oppression and giving a strong voice to marginalized voices.

Tran—Faith Sharings

Tran details how he used faith-sharing as a qualitative research method when writing his doctoral dissertation while studying Catholic detention ministry volunteers. He describes faith-sharing as a more powerful way to share personal spiritual experiences than other data-collection tools. He claims it provides a more authentic connection and reduces power imbalances between the researcher and the participant.

Mooney Simmie—Feminist Discourse Analysis

Mooney Simmie details her research approach, which uses Critical Feminist Discourse Analysis to examine education policy and practice. She uses Critical Pedagogy and Feminist Studies together in her research to explain how power structures and gendered norms have shaped our education systems and moves to advocate for a more ethical approach to education. Mooney Simmie's goal in this approach is to bring about transformative change in education.

Espinosa-Dulanto—Pláticas

Grounded in decolonial and feminist frameworks, *pláticas* create inclusive spaces for storytelling, knowledge creation, and healing, positioning participants as co-creators of meaningful change while addressing broader themes of community and inequality. Pláticas serve as both a methodology and a cultural practice, bridging personal experiences with collective narratives, fostering mutual understanding and community building. As a research method, pláticas disrupt traditional academic structures by centering minoritized voices, emphasizing reciprocity, vulnerability, and reflexivity, and challenging oppressive systems.

Ward—Participatory Action Research (PAR)

Ward explains that Participatory Action Research (PAR) is an epistemological stance emphasizing collaboration and challenging traditional research hierarchies by empowering marginalized voices, as seen in her study involving urban youth. Using arts-based methods, youth co-created data poems and reflected on their complex identities as peer educators, disrupting prevailing narratives about urban youth and embracing a postmodern perspective that values multiple ways of knowing.

Roady—Collective Narrative

Roady's doctoral dissertation discusses collective and co-constructed narrative inquiry as a qualitative research method focusing on collaborative storytelling among participants. This method utilizes building trust and relationships, challenging traditional power dynamics in research, and giving a voice to the marginalized to foster solidarity and counternarratives to the prevalent social structures.

Boucher—Photo Elicitation

Boucher describes photo elicitation as a powerful tool for qualitative research, specifically within critical ethnography. Photo elicitation allows the researcher to use photographs to create a safe environment for the participants to be empowered to share their lived experiences. Photographs are used as tools to promote rich, emotional responses from participants, yielding deeper insights than would traditional interview methods.

Casey—Conclusion: Catalytic Validity

Casey uses catalytic validity occurring before or after an action, where, unlike praxis, an action and reflection can coincide. Casey also positions catalytic validity as an essential framework in critical qualitative research. He stresses that the goal of critical research should be humanizing change, which is only achieved by the participants acting as catalysts for their own transformation.

References

Creswell, J. W., & Poth, C. N. (2016). *Qualitative inquiry and research design: Choosing among five approaches*. SAGE publications.

Higginbotham, E. B. (1994). *Righteous discontent: The women's movement in the Black Baptist church, 1880–1920*. Harvard University Press.

Mertler, C. A. (2021). *Introduction to educational research*. SAGE publications.

Patton, M. Q. (2014). *Qualitative research & evaluation methods: Integrating theory and practice*. SAGE publications.

Ravitch, S. M., & Carl, N. M. (2019). *Qualitative research: Bridging the conceptual, theoretical, and methodological*. SAGE Publications.

ONE

Kanaka ʻŌiwi Methodologies to Honor Moʻōlelo, Communities, Aloha ʻĀina, and Make it Hānai

Robin Brandehoff

What Are ʻŌiwi and "Mixed-Plate" Methodologies That I Use?

In my research to develop my Hānai Pedagogical framework (Brandehoff, 2023b) and scholar identity, I have combined a mix of methodologies which pay homage to the moʻōlelo, kūpuna, and ʻāina of Hawaiʻi, while also recognizing that the population of Hawaiʻi has developed into what one participant lovingly described as *mixed-plate*. This term is in reference to the popular plate lunch combo of foods historically served by and to plantation laborers in Hawaiʻi, representing a rich and diverse background of Native Hawaiians, Japanese, Chinese, Portuguese, Spanish, and other immigrants who traveled to the islands in search of work and a better life after the 1850s.

Much like a mixed-plate lunch, this accumulation of methodologies intentionally combines qualities and intentions of Kanaka ʻŌiwi (Native Hawaiian) culture, proverbs, and mythology, along with the traditions and cultural beliefs of diverse groups stemming from immigrant laborers who crossed vast oceans to live and work together. Collectively, these groups merged and formed their cultures and traditions to produce common protocols such as greetings, ways of discourse, rules about entering houses, and additional ways of knowing, which date back to ancestral teachings that span their lived experiences and diverse nationalities. These same protocols continue to dictate how individuals in Hawaiʻi live and serve today, but also how I established myself as an Asian American and Pacific Islander-identifying researcher, originally from Maui, with insider/outsider privileges on the island (Aikau, 2019), and how I established trust with my participants by becoming a part of the community, rather than just a researcher and observer.

Unfortunately, I did not have the opportunity to live on the island for an extended period of time but would instead take multiple trips back and forth to conduct my interviews and observations within the community and at school sites. Each time, I would spend the better part of the day and night with participants and community members, engaging in conversations, attending local events, reading with children, talking story with kūpuna (elders), and eating with families to learn more about the community and gather *ʻike* (knowledge) through stories (Kahakalau, 2019), local myths, and the ʻāina (land). I did not want to be the researcher who just observed. I wanted to be the researcher whom students came to know and referred to as Anakē (aunty) when I came back to visit. Over a short amount of time, I achieved this level of involvement and commitment within the community, and I was accepted as an insider/outsider member, making future research visits smooth(er), and knowledge sharing became collaborative rather than one-sided.

This connection with the community grounded me with the kanaka and the ʻāina which supported my data collection. In terms of data collection in ʻŌiwi spaces, Kahakalau (2019) advises that the researcher should be knowledgeable in the protocols of Hawaiian and local engagement and conversation before taking part in the research. There are many cultural factors to consider, such as how to address an elder, to kiss an aunty on the cheek, to bring gifts, to take your shoes off outside of the front door, and to be actively engaged during talk story (conversation). The researcher must be a keen observer and willing to share space with partners and elders who hold ancestral knowledge of the ʻāina and kanaka. All of this I knew, as it had settled in my bones from growing up in the islands, but now, as a researcher, I treated these customs with a newfound reverence.

ʻŌiwi methodology includes qualitative data, which is usually collected through informal and conversational narratives locally referred to as talk story (Martin et al., 2023; Watson, 1975). Au and Kawakami (1985) most succinctly describe *talk story* as a joint performance narrative produced by a group of individuals who share their personal experiences as they divulge on a topic. Unlike Western qualitative narratives or *testimonios*, it is not always about one speaker telling their story but an interactive opportunity where others can partake in the action through jokes, responses, and interactions. Historically, talk story is central to ʻŌiwi and Hawaiian islander culture and dates back to plantation laborer history (Lum, 1998; Simpson Steele, 2012).

Generally, this is the best way to gather detailed insight into participant experiences and histories via semi-structured interview questions and probing. These conversations usually take place in homes, backyards, or active spaces fueled by food; they need to be spaced out in a given schedule because some individuals are loquacious and can talk story for a very long time.

During my first research visit, I was working closely with a staff member from INPEACE (Institute for Native Pacific Education and Culture), which is a non-profit community-based organization located on the West side of O'ahu, Hawai'i (which encompasses the largest population of Native Hawaiians in Hawai'i). Their organization has created free educational programming for Native Hawaiian communities since 1994, including early childhood programming with a multigenerational framework to support and educate family members about childcare, education, and resources. Their educational equity sector has a robust teacher development program called Ka Lama, which is the program I partnered with for my research. Through Ka Lama, community members who are interested in teaching can enter into the program and are supported by mentor staff members from INPEACE. They are then provided monetary support through grants and scholarships and are guided through the college and teacher licensing pathway through collaborative efforts with the local community college on the West side of the island. Then, students transfer to a four-year university to complete their degree and become educators and administrators in the state of Hawai'i. Ka Lama and a site principal also trialed a pilot program where the professors from the university ran their classes out of the local elementary school on the West side of the island, which saved students a three-hour round-trip commute to their classes. That pilot class recently graduated with their bachelor's degrees, teaching licenses, and special education certificates, which grant them additional signing bonuses, and they are entering their first year as classroom teachers in the 2024–2025 academic school year.

In our talk story style interviews, I gathered bountiful amounts of knowledge regarding these programs and how Ka Lama has supported teachers throughout their journeys. For educators outside of the pilot program, I learned about their monetary and transportation challenges in getting to their university classes once they transitioned out of the local community college into a four-year university. Yet, from these struggles, they built an ʻohana with their classmates because they formed a carpool schedule, would create study groups at one another's houses, would invite their families over to make childcare manageable, and would encourage one another when classes felt impossible. *Team Hui*, or the pilot class, shared how much they admire their principal and how it was she who pushed them to consider teaching as a career because each of them started off as a paraprofessional in the school and had never considered applying to college until she planted the seed for them. Similarly, these students would also bring their children to the school for classes and would consistently encourage one another through regular check-ins, text messages, and phone calls. Themes of critical mentoring (Morales et al., 2022; Weiston-Serdan, 2017) showed up across all interviews because each participant considered themselves a *non-traditional student* who entered into college later in life or at a socio-economic disadvantage and relied heavily on the mentorship of an INPEACE mentor who racially and/or culturally identified with them and understood 'where they came from' in terms of their background and struggles with finances, family obligations, academic performance, and more.

Disrupting Systems of Oppression and Empowering Participants

'Ōiwi methods not only honor Indigenous ways of knowing (Daniel et al., 2022), but they also humanize the data collection and analysis process by recognizing that the researcher is passionate about their inquiry, has become intricately woven into their community to better understand the phenomenon, and is diving deep into the data through the stories and lived experiences of the actively engaged participants. Talk story as a qualitative data collection method honors the participant's engagement and knowledge basis by committing time, active listening, and participating in a true dialogue with the individual rather than a research interview. It is a method that sets the participant at ease and gives them the floor to share their story while the researcher also engages and participates in the story, and others are able to jump in (if applicable). These stories then become personal, emotional, and tie directly into 'ike and the *mana* or spirit (Kahakalau, 2019), that likely initiated the research in the first place.

Though it is not considered an 'Ōiwi methodology, I have extended the opportunities to participant-check and validate data within my work, particularly with historically marginalized groups (Brandehoff, 2023a; 2024; *in press*). I began this process during my dissertation because I was collaborating with gang-affiliated youth, and I wanted to provide them with an extra layer of protection within their interviews. It was and remains vital to me that I participant-check and collaborate with individuals that I engage with as much as possible, especially if I am conducting case studies on individuals or groups. Once an interview is transcribed, I invite the individual(s) to review their de-identified transcript with the opportunity to redact anything they no longer wish to divulge. I offer this opportunity again after I have completed their section of the case study. As a researcher and co-collaborator, I do not wish to send anything out into the world without their blessing. During my dissertation process, this extra layer provided additional opportunities for participants to review their words and how I interpreted and wrote about their experiences, and gave them the chance to change it. To date, no participant has opted to change or redact information from their transcripts or from my case study write ups, but I believe that these member-checking measures are important to the methodology and analysis process because I do not ever want to assume that my interpretation of another individual's experience(s) is correct. In offering this review process, I am empowering participants to say "no," to remove themselves from the study, or to change their narrative, and this is important to me because I do not want any individual to ever regret sharing information in an interview.

In my current research in Hawai'i, I have conducted work based on my pedagogical framework, Hānai Pedagogy (Brandehoff, 2023b), and I have continued this participant-checking process. Though the research is not considered "action research," I aim for it to be collaborative, and I use 'Ōiwi methodologies and qualities of Mā'awe Pono (Kahakalau, 2019) to conduct my data collection through talk story (Martin et al., 2023; Watson, 1975) to fully encompass the experiences of those who share their stories and knowledge with me. Perhaps one of my favorite moments from this study (to date) has been participant-checking the name of the framework with my participants. Hānai is closely translated to adopted kin, and from my interactions, observations, and talk stories, I learned that the pedagogy of these classrooms was akin to 'ohana spaces where the teacher was more like an aunty or uncle and the children were connected like cousins. The learning is taught through talk story—with a mixture of local mythology and US standards, spoken through pidgin dialect that students are comfortable with. Hānai also became an acronym for the five principles of the framework, which include: Hands-on learning, Aloha (love), Navigation, Authenticity, and Interrelations (Brandehoff, 2023b). As I shared this with each participant, each and every participant smiled and nodded like a blessing. They understood its importance and foundation and appreciated its nuance rooted in the stories and experiences they each shared with me.

Foundational Texts and Important Theorists

Kanaka ʻŌiwi methodologies intentionally honor ancestors, traditions, and culture, and vary across the literature but share many parallels with other Indigenous forms of methodologies (Smith, 2021). The top scholars to examine would include Jonathan Kay Kamakawiwoʻole Osorio (2004), whose work examines the history of Hawaiʻi and specifically how we connect with our ancestors, while the individual and collaborative scholarship of Erin Kahunawaikaʻala Wright (2017), Noelani Goodyear-Kaʻōpua (2016), and Katrina-Ann R. Kapāʻanaokalāokeloa Nākoa Oliveira (2017) take a feminist stance to the history and future of higher education in Hawaiʻi and how ʻŌiwi research can navigate both collaboration and independence in the academy.

These scholars have woven the foundation for the two books highlighted in this chapter, including Oliveira and Wright's (2017) *Kanaka ʻŌiwi Methodologies: Moʻolelo and Metaphor*, which includes Goodyear-Kaʻōpua's (2016) Methodological Ropes for Research and Resurgence. This chapter highlights the principles of "Lāhui (collective identity and self-definition), ea (sovereignty and leadership), kuleana (positionality and obligations), and pono (harmonious relationships, justice, and healing)" (p. 2) to build community and collaboration with participants and co-produce our knowledge collaboratively. As a researcher, guided by my epistemological roots in the islands, I have been equally guided by Wilson-Hokowhitu's (2019) edited book *The Past Before Us: Moʻokūʻauhau as Methodology*, which is a collection of chapters from practitioner scholars using genealogy as methodology to explore scholarship and honor research through ʻŌiwi theory and practice.

In my most recent work with doctoral students, which centers critical mentoring and our parallel epistemologies, I have been heavily influenced by the qualities of Kahakalau's (2019) Māʻawe Pono methodological framework, which centers the researcher and their *mana*, or spiritual power. Mana guides the research process and encourages the researcher to become intrinsically involved within the community or space of research to better understand the phenomenon. As I mentioned earlier, this process takes time and active involvement within the community of research, which means the researcher must take the time to get to know the community beyond just the participants in order to become part of the community and allow "ancestral *ʻike* (knowledge) and recent insight to interact and surface as new knowledge" (Kahakalau, 2019, p. 14).

In traditional Western research, this form of methodology may be consistent with ethnography (Van Maanen, 1988), where the researcher becomes a long-time observer of the community and phenomenon of inquiry. At times, the researcher may interact with the community members and live among them to gain more insight, but as I mentioned earlier, it is also about becoming intrinsically involved within the fabric of the community and to become *Hānai*. These methods share parallels with Western research in the academy, but they also extend learning and knowing to honor the experiences, the participants, and the histories of *ʻāina* in nuanced ways that are empowering and spiritual. These methods provide a third space for the researcher and participant to step back in time to explore *moʻokūʻauhau* (genealogy) and all its connections, when little else mattered but the moʻōlelo, the company around you, and the lessons you took away from kūpuna's story that night.

Suggestions for Further Reading and References

Aikau, H. K. (2019). From malihini to hoaʻāina: Reconnecting people, places, and practices. In N. Wilson-Hokuwhitu (Ed.), *The past before us: Moʻokū ʻauhau as methodology* (pp. 81–91). University of Hawaii Press.

Au, K. H., & Kawakami, A. J. (1985). Research currents: Talk story and learning to read. *Language Arts, 62*(4), 406–411.

Brandehoff, R. (2023a). The ripple effect of mentorship: A cross-case analysis of five rural, Latine youth. *Journal of Latinos and Education*, 1–16. https://www.tandfonline.com/eprint/EXA8FSKMEMXADXPTJY6I/full?target=10.1080/15348431.2023.2258198

Brandehoff, R. (2023b). Introducing Hānai pedagogy: A call for equity in education through an AANAPI lens. *Pedagogy and Theatre of the Oppressed Journal, 7*(1), 1–15.

Brandehoff, R. (2024). One moment, two plates of food: Dismantling the carceral education pipeline through mentorship. *About Campus: Enriching the Student Learning Experience, 29(4)*, 25–34. https://doi.org/10.1177/10864822241252179.

Brandehoff, R. (in press). Humanizing the multiple case study experience: An exploration of informal mentorships among Latiné, gang-affiliated youth. *Sage Research Methods Data and Scientific Literacy*: SAGE.

Daniel, R. A., Wilhelm, T. A., Case-Scott, H., Goldman, G., & Hinzman, L. (2022, December 2). What is "Indigenous knowledge" and why does it matter? Integrating ancestral wisdom and approaches into federal decision making." *The White House*. https://www.whitehouse.gov/ostp/news-updates/2022/12/02/what-is-indigenous-knowledge-and-why-does-it-matter-integrating-ancestral-wisdom-and-approaches-into-federal-decision-making/

Goodyear-Ka'ōpua, N. (2016). Reproducing the ropes of resistance: Hawaiian studies methodologies. In K. A. R. K. A. N. Oliveira, & E. K. A. Wright, (Eds.), *Kanaka 'Ōiwi methodologies: Mo'olelo and metaphor* (pp. 1–29). University of Hawaii Press.

Kahakalau, K. (2019). Māʻawe Pono: Treading on the trail of honor and responsibility. In N. Wilson-Hokuwhitu (Ed.) *The past before us: Mo'okū 'auhau as methodology* (pp. 9–27). University of Hawaii Press.

Lum, D. (1998). Local genealogy: What school you went? In E. Chock (Ed.), *Growing up local: An anthology of poetry and prose from Hawaii* (pp. 11–15). Bamboo Ridge Press.

Martin, T. K. K., Merculief, A., Young, R. I., White, L., Marshall, S. M., Waubanascum, C., White, E. J., & Russette, H. (2023). Striving to be pono (balanced, equitable, and hopeful): Conceptualizing an Indigenous writing process from a Native Hawaiian cultural perspective. *Adversity and Resilience Science, 4*(1), 435–458. https://doi.org/10.1007/s42844-023-00121-0

Morales, A. R., Espinoza, P. S., & Duke, K. B. (2022). What exists and what I need: In search of critical, empowering, and race-conscious approaches to mentoring from the perspective of Latina/o/x teachers. In C. D. Gist, & T. J. Bristol, (Eds.), *Handbook of research on teachers of color and Indigenous teachers* (pp. 441–458).

Oliveira, K. A. R. K. A. N., & Wright, E. K. A. (Eds.). (2017). *Kanaka 'Ōiwi methodologies: Mo'olelo and metaphor*. University of Hawaii Press.

Osorio, J. K. K. O. (2004). Gazing back: Communing with our ancestors. *Educational Perspectives, 37*(1), 14–17.

Reyes, N. A. S., Wright, E. K., Goodyear-Ka'ōpua, N., & Oliveira, K. A. R. K. N. (2019). Embodying Haumea: Wāhine scholars cultivating Kanaka independence/ts in the academy. *International Journal of Qualitative Studies in Education, 33*(2), 240–249. https://doi.org/10.1080/09518398.2019.1681543

Simpson Steele, J. (2012). Talk-story: A quest for new research methodology in neocolonial Hawai'i. *Youth Theatre Journal, 26*(1), 38–49. https://doiorg.aurarialibrary.idm.oclc.org/10.1080/08929092.2012.678213

Smith, L. T. (2021). *Decolonizing methodologies: Research and Indigenous peoples*. Bloomsbury Publishing.

Van Maanen, J. (1988). *Tales of the field: On writing ethnography*. University of Chicago Press.

Watson, K. A. (1975). Transferable communicative routines: Strategies and group identity in two speech events. *Language in Society, 4*(1), 53–72.

Weiston-Serdan, T. (2017). *Critical mentoring: A practical guide*. Stylus Publishing.

Wilson-Hokowhitu, N. (Ed.). (2019). *The past before us: Mo'okū'auhau as methodology*. University of Hawaii Press.

Wright, E. K. (2017). Reclaiming Indigenous Research in Higher Education. In R. S. M. & H. J. Shotton (Ed.), *Reclaiming Indigenous research in higher education* (pp. 18–35). Rutgers University Press.

Chapter 1 Discussion Questions

1. How does incorporating 'Ōiwi methodologies, such as talk story and community engagement protocols, differ from Western qualitative research approaches?
2. Brandehoff emphasizes becoming an insider/outsider within the Hawaiian community to build trust. What strategies did they employ to achieve this status, and how might these strategies be adapted for other contexts in educational research?
3. The Ka Lama program emphasizes mentorship and community-based support for aspiring educators. How do programs such as this address systemic barriers in education, and what lessons can be drawn for creating similar initiatives in other underrepresented communities?
4. Brandehoff highlights participant-checking as a key ethical practice in their study. How does this practice contribute to empowering participants, and what challenges might arise when implementing member checking in qualitative research?

TWO

Anticolonial Ethics in Critical Qualitative Research

Lorien S. Jordan

What Is Anticolonial Ethics?

AN ANTICOLONIAL ETHICAL PRAXIS PUSHES beyond the narrow institutional framework of research ethics commonly taught and practiced in the United States. *Anticolonialism* comprises an expansive variety and history of resistance movements against imperial and colonial powers (Dei, 2006). It is a vital project, considering that nearly all nations have been colonized or were colonial powers, and only four countries escaped subjugation to European colonial rule or influence (Blakemore, 2024). Within the social sciences, anticolonialism is "broadly defined as a theoretical framework, analytical tool, and grounded, place-based practice oriented toward resisting, fighting against, and dismantling the aims of colonial regimes, systems, and ideologies" (Nunn & Whetung, 2020, p. 1).

Colonialism is a process comprising different typologies, (e.g., extractive, neo, and settler) (Jordan & Hall, 2023), wherein one power pursues, exerts, and sustains dominance over another through human, land, and resource exploitation (Loomba, 2002). The *sciences* are complicit in colonialism (Jordan, 2022a), using them to justify and stoke colonialism's violence through the imperial doctrine of discovery. Imperialism is a governing ethos of European colonialism, which, as Smith (2021) wrote, "enabled European nations to imagine the possibility that new worlds, new wealth and new possessions existed that could be discovered and controlled. This imagination was realized through the promotion of science" (p. 25). The imperial imagination has evolved into a contemporary ethos that engenders unequal power relations in science, wherein the knowledge, philosophies, methodologies, and theories of the *West* are canonized—deemed universal, objective, rational, and acultural (Jordan & Hall, 2023), ensuring the inferiority of any other truth or method of knowing (Kilomba, 2010).

In contemporary education research ethics, a Euro-American onto-epistemological lens promoting individualism (Denzin, 2009) guides federally mandated standards of practice and discipline-specific codes of conduct, often "reduced to the discussion of securing approval from an Institutional Review Board (IRB)" (Tuck & Guishard, 2013, p. 4). However, the IRB's regulatory procedures enshrine the interests and liabilities of universities steeped in histories of "wealth accumulation through slavery and Indigenous land dispossession" (Sabati, 2019, p. 1057). Sole reliance on the IRB and Euro-American ethics can reproduce settler colonial and white supremacist ideologies. Further, teaching ethics from this standpoint does little to instill an understanding of the colonial entanglements of knowledge production and our academic disciplines (Patel, 2016).

To confront this evasion, I teach and practice anticolonial ethical praxis. Given the fluid dimensions of anticolonial ethics and the responsibility of disrupting the status quo in research, I embrace ethics as a praxis. An anticolonial ethical praxis aims "at rehumanising the world, redistributing resources and producing counter-knowledges and counter-praxes" to hold "accountable Eurocentric and patriarchal ways of being, doing, thinking and relating in order to imagine and build alternative worlds, presents and futures" (Castillo, 2023, p. 23). In the following, I explore four principles of praxis that guide my research and pedagogy. These principles describe the interconnected relationships between our thinking (theorizing), acting (method/ology), reflecting (reflexivity), and relating (answerability). These principles should be considered vis-à-vis one another, building on and informing the next in a mutual cycle of generativity.

Thinking and Theorizing

Foundational to anticolonial ethical praxis is developing knowledge of how the sciences, institutions, and disciplines are colonially complicit, including how our research practices are embedded in colonial knowledge production (Sabati, 2019). Ethics in education research framed on Euro-American ideas about the primacy of the individual has led to the commodification of knowledge (Denzin, 2009). Rarely included is a discussion of how contemporary research approaches are distilled from practices that dehumanized and Othered the colonized to signify the supremacy of the colonizers (Tuck &

Guishard, 2013). This distillation is apparent when we consider how we claim to *give voice* when working with *marginalized* or *hard-to-reach* communities. These damage-centered portraits of communities create deficit-centered and pathologized knowledge that, in turn, suggests that certain communities are researchable and that we are uniquely entitled to study them (Tuck, 2009).

Anticolonial ethics provokes deep reading and reflecting on our academic institutions (Stein, 2020), onto-epistemologies and research practices (Smith, 2021), ethics (Denzin, 2009), and the education discipline (Patel, 2016). Similarly, the theories critical of coloniality also provide a foundation from which to begin an anticolonial praxis, including anticolonialism (Dei, 2006), decoloniality (Mignolo, 2011), decolonization (Smith, 2021), settler colonialism (Veracini, 2010) and postcolonialism (Loomba, 2002). This involves looking to works of scholars who may have been silenced, acknowledging the contributions of artists and activists, bringing diverse onto-epistemologies into conversation, and critically navigating complex issues of power in the production of knowledge.

Reflecting and Reflexivity

An anticolonial ethical praxis requires the practice of critical self-reflexivity (Jordan, 2022b). Criticality invites us beyond oversimplified expressions of our social locations or identifying as insiders or outsiders. We have power as researchers regardless of our social identities, privileges and oppressions, and community belongingness. As we learn about imperialism in our disciplines, we commit to reflecting on our positionality within colonialism and how we orient to complicity in its continuance or solidarity in its disruption.

To begin this journey, we can learn the histories of the spaces and places we work, the lands we call home, and how we have come to be a part of and know these places (see Jordan, 2022b). We can also examine our role in colonizing academic agendas, considering how we situate ourselves as *the knower* and communities as *known*, reflecting on Kilomba's (2010) questioning: "What knowledge has been made part of academic agendas? And what knowledge has not? Whose knowledge is this? Who is acknowledged to have the knowledge? And who is not? Who can teach knowledge? And who cannot? Who inhabits the academia? And who remains outside at the margins? And finally, who can speak?" (p. 27). These questions lead to others: How did I become entitled to speak for others? How did I gain this power?

Anticolonial reflexivity requires that we remain flexible and open to revising our research designs, questions, and interpretations as a project unfolds. Most importantly, it calls attention to the transformative impact of research on the researcher, echoing Wilson's (2008) provocation: "If research hasn't changed you as a person, then you haven't done it right" (p. 135).

Acting and Method/ology

When we teach methodologies from texts that narrowly describe a handful of approaches, we edify the white, Euro-American, extractive, and disembodying methods as *the* way to research. Instead, an anticolonial ethical praxis acts against canonization by valuing multiple pathways of knowledge development and the expertise of many communities to interrupt "knowledge hierarchies" (Tuck & Guishard, 2013, p. 18). However, Audre Lorde (2012) warned that "the master's tools will never dismantle the master's house" (p. 112). In response, Smith (2021) wrote that the challenge is "to fashion new tools" (p. 60). This challenge speaks to the anticolonial ethical praxis of action through embracing tools that integrate experiential and traditionally Other(ed) ways of knowing into our designs, countering methodological canonization.

There are many examples of anticolonial method/ologies that center the "interconnectivity between human, animals, nature, oppression, liberation, pain, joy, laughter, and whimsy" (Bhattacharya, 2021, p. 182), including contemplative and healing (Morton et al., 2021), oral and testimonial (Anzaldúa, 2015). Arts-based, embodied, and playful approaches push beyond linguistic and extractive methods (Jordan et al., in press). Methodologies move beyond resistance, centering on non-oppositional, limitless, and connected knowledge (Keating, 2012). Powerfully, we can engage in participatory projects that involve community members meaningfully throughout all research stages (Tuck & Guishard, 2013), including methodologies of place (see Tuck & McKenzie, 2014). Ultimately, ethical acting means considering what good the research produces beyond short-term dissemination and focusing on the long-term reciprocity to the knowledge bearers (e.g., participants) we work with (Tuck & Guishard, 2013).

Relating and Answerability

Anticolonial ethical praxis resides in foregrounding relationships in our research, illustrated by Kovach's (2015) statement that "research, like life, is about relationships" (p. 55). Accountable relationships evoke a feeling of responsibility for our actions, recognizing that these actions are not isolated, but in relation to all living things, land, and the cosmos. They include the dynamic relations among researchers, participants, context, communities, and the knowledge built (Wilson, 2008).

Patel (2016) depicted relationality as being answerable, "responsible, accountable, and being part of an exchange. It is a concept that can help to maintain the coming-into-being with, being in conversation with" (p. 73) knowledge. Answerability asks us to interact ethically, not just in the research encounter but in our relational roles across time and context, including the legacy of colonialism and the refusal to sustain it (Patel, 2016). Relationality is our remaining answerable for the knowledge we develop and the far-reaching and fluid consequences and permutations it might take. To catalyze answerability in our research relations, we can consider how we might answer questions posed by Wilson (2008), including:

> How can I relate respectfully to the other participants involved in this research so that together we can form a stronger relationship with the idea that we will share? Am I being responsible in fulfilling my role and obligations to the other participants, to the topic and to all of my relations? What am I contributing or giving back to the relationship? Is the sharing, growth, and learning that is taking place reciprocal? (p. 77)

Anticolonial Ethical Praxis in Action

The classroom can be a site of anticolonial resistance, and in my introductory qualitative courses, I teach ethics via the four principles of anticolonial praxis. First, students are invited to *think and theorize*, reading texts on the colonial legacy of institutional ethics (Denzin, 2009; Sabati, 2019; Tuck & Guishard, 2013). After discussing these readings on the day of class, I invite the students to engage in an activity that integrates *action*, *reflection*, and *relating*.

As described above, methodological action involves experiential methods typically excluded from the Euro-American canon. Modeling this spirit, students participate in a modified body-mapping activity (Morton et al., 2021). Body-mapping asks participants to create tracings of their bodies, which they then illustrate to narrate their sensory, bodily, and intuitive experiences. Teaching anticolonial ethics through body-mapping shifts learning from the mind-body dualism common in Euro-American practices and asks students to connect knowledge, experience, self, soul, other, and world (Morton et al., 2021).

Acknowledging the mind-body connection, I first engage students in a grounding meditation to promote a reflective state of being while acknowledging that the activity might bring up difficult emotions (see Magee, 2021 for possible meditations). Then, I pass out a handout of a genderless human form and a box of markers before playing Linda Tuhiwai Smith's (2019) poem, *Research Ethics and Indigenous Peoples 101*. This poem evocatively provokes reflection and theorizing, explicitly painting the history of harm enacted by scientists in the name of *civilization*.

Students then engage in reflective action by illustrating their response to the poem, following the body-mapping method, using symbols, figures, markings, images, words, and colors placed strategically on their body-maps. I invite students to begin their reflections with prompts such as: *What kind of symbols, figures, or images reflect the central message you took from this poem, and your experience of hearing it? Where would you place these images in, on, or outside your body? Looking from head to toe, do any of the specific marks you made provoke concern for you in thinking about conducting research?*

After peer discussion of their maps, we think about our relational answerability using Smith's (2019) poem as a springboard. Students return to their maps, illustrating where they find hope and strength to disrupt injustice through research, what relations help them carry this strength, and how they can ethically connect to all their research relations. For example, some prompts I offer the students include: *Think about a symbol or image that captures what you hope your future as a researcher holds for you. Draw this symbol on your body-map to represent the fulfillment you are striving for. How could you represent the kind of relationship you have, or hope to have, with your participants/communities? Reflect on the hope or strength you hold that we can disrupt power and control through our research relations. What is a symbol that you could draw or a word you could use to describe this hope and strength?*

Where would you put it on your body to carry, to indicate how and where you carry it into the world?

In teaching ethics through an anticolonial lens, I aim to light a spark or fan the flames within students to recognize that the task of anticolonial ethics is each of ours, not just that of critical scholars or scholars of Indigeneity, because we are all trained in, work under, and develop knowledge imbued in colonial legacies.

Disrupting Systems of Oppression and Empowering Participants

Euro-American imperialism has co-opted the construction of knowledge, building the academy and research practices from onto-epistemological frameworks that benefit and normalize white, hetero-patriarchal, ableist systems of power. As the beneficiaries of these systems, education researchers are called to disrupt systems of oppression, working as "practitioners committed to truth and knowledge production," recognizing that "institutional commitments to anticolonial and antiracist research should not be matters of theoretical orientation, but matters of practicing better social inquiry" (Sabati, 2019, p. 1061). This commitment spurs anticolonial ethics, situating at its center the interrogation and denouncement of colonial practices and ideologies while advocating for Other(ed) ways of knowing.

Historically, education research has focused on studying communities labeled as *disadvantaged* or *marginalized*, aiming to *fix* these communities, bringing them in line with standards determined by white, Euro-American society (Walsdorf et al., 2020).

This colonial research agenda perpetrates epistemological violence and epistemic injustice (Jordan & Hall, 2023). Epistemological violence (Teo, 2010) occurs when data are interrupted to problematize or make inferior the Other. For example, epistemological violence occurs in *achievement gaps* research, which sustains the discourse of *students as failures* (Carey, 2014) rather than on how colonialism requires these failures (Tuck & Guishard, 2013). Epistemic injustice is the inequity of who gets to know and what is believed to be knowledge, provoking questions of how academics exclude and silence people from developing experiential knowledge (Kidd et al., 2017). Epistemic injustice occurs throughout the education system, including in the fight against critical race theory (Jordan et al., 2024), whose detractors seek to subjugate and silence testimony of racism while also diminishing a theoretical and methodological orientation developed from those who live racism's consequences.

Both epistemic injustice and epistemological violence are perpetrated against people whose social identities are devalued based on colonial-ideological categories of race, gender, sexuality, class, nationality, religion, and ability (Jordan, 2021). Therefore, enacting an anticolonial praxis means not just focusing on race or Indigeneity but all powers and categories that seek to dehumanize and oppress. This focus includes exploring the coloniality of the hypotheses and questions they set out to explore, considerations of who is able and trusted to speak, and why scholars claim to be able to speak for or *give voice* to communities. It means embracing liberatory, experiential, and creative ways of knowing and being, arriving at conclusions embraced as legitimate because they come from those who have the experiential knowledge, not despite it. Above all, an anticolonial ethical praxis is a humanizing endeavor that strikes "at the very heart of dominant ideologies linked to persistent asymmetrical practices—practices that, wittingly or unwittingly, reproduce classed, racialized, gendered, heterosexual, abled, religious, and other formations that sustain recalcitrant inequalities, intractable social exclusions, and the persisting political disaffiliation of the subaltern" (Darder, 2018, p. 96).

Foundational Texts and Theorists

Anticolonialism is integral to colonialism's story, and since the first colonial contact, people have resisted and opposed its violence and control. Accordingly, many anticolonial movements evoke research agendas that interrogate and counter the imperial logic of Euro-American centricity. Given the range of anticolonial scholarships, I share foundational authors who have aided in my ongoing "unsettling."

Linda Tuhiwai Smith (Ngāti Awa, Ngāti Porou, Tūhourangi) and her groundbreaking text, *Decolonizing Methodologies*, critically analyzed imperial science's role in historical and contemporary colonization. While Smith's (2021) intended audience was Indigenous scholars, it has influenced a global audience that includes Indigenous and non-Indigenous researchers' paths toward reconsidering their means, modes, and methods of research. Smith

(2021) opens the book by drawing attention to the complicated relationship that Indigenous scholars have to inquiry, writing. . . . "The word itself, 're-search,' is probably one of the dirtiest words in the Indigenous world's vocabulary" (p. 1). She first describes imperial science's violence before outlining several decolonizing research principles. Smith (2021) illustrates decolonizing as a theory in action, providing many examples of decolonizing and Indigenous projects, depicting research grounded in Indigenous self-determination and sovereignty.

In education, Eve Tuck's (Unangax̂) influential scholarship has brought concepts of resistance and settler colonialism into conversation with diverse issues from curriculum to student experiences, theories of change, and the centrality of place (Tuck & McKenzie, 2014). Tuck's significant contributions to the conceptualizations and practice of research ethics have led to several articles challenging ideas of what it means to do justice-oriented work. Her article *Suspending Damage* (Tuck, 2009) emphasizes how well-intentioned researchers continue to portray communities as inherently damaged, suggesting instead that we focus on desire. Tuck and Yang's (2014) classic piece, *Decolonization is not a Metaphor*, critiques the use of decolonizing by settler academics wishing to reconcile their complicity in settler colonialism.

Lorenzo Veracini (2010) is a significant voice in settler colonial theory (SCT). Central to my understanding of and commitment to anticolonialism is his critical analysis of the naturalization of the white settler. SCT illustrates how settlers in what became the United States created whiteness to justify their violence and genocide against those marked as *uncivilized* (e.g., Indigenous) and *savage* (e.g., exogenous persons such as the enslaved and immigrants). Through this process, white settlers made themselves the norm, and "by naturalizing whiteness, the English language, Christianity, binary genders, and ablebodiedness, the image of the indigenized American has become embedded in the fabric of the nation" (Jordan & Dykes, 2022, p. 4). Naturalized to the United States, white settlers justify violence against those who threaten their sovereignty. Such violence is seen today in the police and civilian vigilantism against Black and Brown people and the collective violence on display during the January 6th insurrection (Jordan & Dykes, 2022). Veracini's SCT weaves together such narratives of settling, illustrating how settling is a perpetual structure in the US and one that education researchers can confront through anticolonial resistance.

Suggestions for Further Reading

Carlson, E. (2016). Anti-colonial methodologies and practices for settler colonial studies. *Settler Colonial Studies, 7*(4), 496–517. http://dx.doi.org/10.1080/2201473X.2016.1241213

Coddington, K. (2017). Voice under scrutiny: Feminist methods, anticolonial responses, and new methodological tools. *The Professional Geographer, 69*(2), 314–320. https://doi.org/10.1080/00330124.2016.1208512

Datta, R. (2018). Decolonizing both researcher and research and its effectiveness in Indigenous research. *Research Ethics, 14*(2), 1–24. https://doi.org/10.1177/1747016117733296

de Sousa Santos, B. (2015). *Epistemologies of the South: Justice against epistemicide.* Routledge.

Kempf, A. (Ed.). (2009). *Breaching the colonial contract: Anti-colonialism in the US and Canada.* Springer Science & Business Media.

Maldonado-Torres, N. (2016). Colonialism, neocolonial, internal colonialism, the postcolonial, coloniality, and decoloniality. In Y. Martínez-San Miguel, B. Sifuentes-Jáuregui & M. Belausteguigoitia (Eds.). *Critical terms in Caribbean and Latin American thought* (pp. 67–78). Palgrave Macmillan, New York.

Spivak, G. C. (2015). Can the subaltern speak? In P. Williams & L. Chrisman. *Colonial discourse and post-colonial theory: A reader* (pp. 64–111). Routledge

References

Anzaldúa, G. (2015). *Light in the dark/Luz en lo oscuro: Rewriting identity, spirituality, reality.* Duke University Press.

Bhattacharya, K. (2021). Rejecting labels and colonization: In exile from post-qualitative approaches. *Qualitative Inquiry, 27*(2), 179–184.

Blakemore, E. (2024). Colonialism facts and information. *National Geographic.* https://www.nationalgeographic.com/culture/article/colonialism

Carey, R. L. (2014). A cultural analysis of the achievement gap discourse: Challenging the language and labels used in the work of school reform. *Urban Education, 49*(4), 440–468.

Castillo, R. C. A. (2023). Critical research ethics as decolonial praxis: Current debates. *International Quarterly for Asian Studies, 54*(1), 21–37.

Darder, A. (2018). Decolonizing interpretive research: Subaltern sensibilities and the politics of voice. *Qualitative Research Journal, 18*(2), 94–104. https://doi.org/10.1108/QRJ-D-17-00056

Dei, G. S. (2006). Mapping the terrain—towards a new politics of resistance. In G. S. Dei & A. Kempf (Eds), *Anti-colonialism and education: The politics of resistance* (pp. 1–23). Sense.

Denzin, N. K. (2009). *Qualitative inquiry under fire: Toward a new paradigm dialogue.* Routledge.

Jordan, L. S., (2021). Belonging and otherness: The violability and complicity of settler colonial sexual violence. *Women & Therapy, 44*(3–4), 271–291.

Jordan, L. S. (2022a). Unsettling the family sciences: Introducing settler colonial theory through a theoretical analysis of the family and racialized injustice. *Journal of Family Theory and Review, 14*(3), 463–481.

Jordan, L. S. (2022b). Unsettling colonial mentalities in family therapy: Entering negotiated spaces. *Journal of Family Therapy, 44*(1), 171–185.

Jordan L. S., Dykes, D. (2022). "If you don't fight like hell, you're not going to have a country": An intersectional settler colonial analysis of Trump's "Save America" speech and other messages of (nonbelonging). *Cultural Studies—Critical Methodologies. 22*(5), 443–453.

Jordan, L. S. & Hall, J. N. (2023). Framing anticolonialism in evaluation: Bridging decolonizing methodologies and culturally responsive evaluation. *Journal of MultiDisciplinary Evaluation, 19*(44), 102–116.

Jordan, L. S., Piontak, R. R., Treco, K. & McKoy, S. (2024). Enwhitened spaces: A critical race/critical whiteness content analysis of whiteness, disinformation, and Amazon reviews. *Thresholds in Education, 47*(1), 69–87. https://academyforeducationalstudies.org/wp-content/uploads/2024/05/jordan-et-al.pdf

Jordan, L. S., Smirnova, D., & Gonzalez-Pliss, A. (in press). Arts-based research. In B. Bell & A. Anders (Eds). *Routledge handbook of research methodologies and methods in social sciences.* Routledge.

Keating, A. (2012). *Transformation now!: Toward a post-oppositional politics of change.* University of Illinois Press.

Kidd, I. J., Medina, J., & Pohlhaus, Jr. G. (2017). *The Routledge handbook of epistemic injustice.* Routledge.

Kilomba, G. (2010). *Plantation memories. Episodes of everyday racism (2nd ed.).* Unrast.

Kovach, M. (2015). Emerging from the margins: Indigenous methodologies. In L. A. Brown & S. Strega (Eds.), *Research as resistance: Revisiting critical, indigenous, and anti-oppressive approaches* (pp. 43–64). Canadian Scholars' Press: Women's Press.

Loomba, A. (2002). *Colonialism/postcolonialism.* Routledge.

Lorde, A. (2012). *Sister outsider: Essays and speeches* (3rd ed.). Crossing Press.

Magee, R. V. (2021). *The inner work of racial justice: Healing ourselves and transforming our communities through mindfulness.* Penguin.

Mignolo, W. (2011). *The darker side of western modernity: Global futures, decolonial options.* Duke University Press.

Morton, D., Bird-Naytowhow, K., & Hatala, A. R. (2021). Silent voices, absent bodies, and quiet methods: revisiting the processes and outcomes of personal knowledge production through Body-Mapping methodologies among Indigenous youth. *International Journal of Qualitative Methods, 20*, 1–14. https://doi.org/10.1177/1609406920987934.

Nunn, N., & Whetung, M. (2020). Anticolonialism. In A. Kobayashi (Ed). *International Encyclopedia of Human Geography* (pp. 155–158). Elsevier.

Patel, L. (2016). *Decolonizing educational research: From ownership to answerability.* Routledge.

Sabati, S. (2019). Upholding "colonial unknowing" through the IRB: Reframing institutional research ethics. *Qualitative Inquiry, 25*(9-10), 1056–1064.

Smith, L. T. (2019). *Research ethics and Indigenous peoples 101* [Video recording]. The Sociological Review. https://www.youtube.com/watch?v=YSX_4FnqXwQ&t=144s.

Smith, L. T. (2021). *Decolonizing methodologies: Research and Indigenous peoples* (3rd ed.). Zed Books.

Stein, S. (2020). A colonial history of the higher education present: Rethinking land-grant institutions through processes of accumulation and relations of conquest. *Critical Studies in Education, 61*(2), 212–228.

Teo, T. (2010). What is epistemological violence in the empirical social sciences? *Social and Personality Psychology Compass, 4*(5), 295–303. https://doi.org/10.1111/j.1751-9004.2010.00265.x

Tuck E. (2009). Suspending damage: A letter to communities. *Harvard Educational Review, 79*, 409–428.

Tuck E., & Guishard M. (2013). Uncollapsing ethics: Racialized sciencism, settler coloniality, and an ethical framework of decolonial participatory action research. In T. M. Kress, C. Malott, B. J. Porfilio (Eds.). *Challenging status quo retrenchment: New directions in critical research* (pp. 3–27). Information Age.

Tuck, E., & McKenzie, M. (2014). *Place in research: Theory, methodology, and methods.* Routledge.

Tuck, E., & Yang, K. W. (2014). Decolonization is not a metaphor. *Decolonization: Indigeneity, Education and Society, 1*(1), 1–40.

Walsdorf, A. A., Jordan, L. S., McGeorge, C. R., & Caughy, M. O. (2020). White supremacy and the web of family science: Implications of the missing spider. *Journal of Family Theory & Review, 12*(1), 64–79.

Wilson, S. (2008). *Research is ceremony: Indigenous research methods.* Fernwood Publishing.

Veracini, L. (2010). *Settler colonialism.* Palgrave Macmillan.

Chapter 2 Discussion Questions

1. How can the principles of anticolonial ethical praxis challenge and reshape the way researchers approach marginalized communities in education research? Reflect on how traditional methods may unintentionally perpetuate epistemological violence or epistemic injustice.
2. Considering Kilomba's and Patel's questions about who holds power in academic knowledge production, discuss how researchers might navigate their positionality to avoid reproducing colonial systems of power and privilege in their work. What practical steps can researchers take to embrace *answerability*?
3. Jordan discusses methodologies, such as body mapping and participatory designs, that counter the dominance of Euro-American traditions in research. What are the potential challenges to and benefits of incorporating such methods into academic research? How can these approaches contribute to disrupting *knowledge hierarchies*?
4. Reflect on the example of teaching ethics through body-mapping described in the chapter. How might this activity influence students' understanding of relational and ethical responsibility in research? What other pedagogical strategies could foster similar awareness and commitment to anticolonial principles?

THREE

The Art of Creative Resourcefulness: Rasquache as Methodology

Jasmin Patrón-Vargas and Tim Monreal

Jasmin: *Just finished reading your paper . . . We [too] definitely use[d] old clothes as cleaning rags* 🤣 *[So] After we introduce ourselves show the video, maybe u can kick off with a question like this* 😂

Tim: 🙌🙌 *Then we can show pictures and work through our paper? I'm cool to adlib it out in the [Zoom] chat as we go* 🤣🤣

Jasmin: 😆 *I'm down. I'll throw some pics in the handout so we can use it as [a] reference (referring to a handout we created for this guest lecture). . . . So many memories and things to unpack in these photos. I love to see it and can't wait to dig into it*

Tim: *Another piece we need to write about is the ability of rasquache to reclaim joy and laughter* 🙂

Jasmin: *Yes!!! I was thinking that. The ways this allows us to (re)member and reclaim joy in a playful way. That could be another one in community with students, perhaps.* 😃

We are two unapologetic rasquacherxs who make the most of the tools we have (Gonzales, 2022; Medina López, 2017; Monreal, 2021). The excerpt above is from a previous text message conversation between the two of us. Using a blend of professional and social dialogue that mirrors *rasquache* (pronounced *ras-kwa-che*) movidas (individual maneuvers/moves) of simultaneous irreverence and seriousness, we used our digital chat (excerpted above) to finalize the main points of a guest lecture later that day. Inadvertently, through our informal plática and discussion of the guest lecture, we begin planting seeds for this longer meditation on *rasquache/rasquachismx* (as) methodology. By providing a glimpse of our methodological process, we hope to empower students, instructors, and novice scholars to engage innovative methodological approaches with whatever is on hand. Thus, we aim to share how methodology/ies might revel in and create knowledge from *nuestras chingaderas*, movidas, and scrappiness.

In this chapter, we identify the contours of rasquache methodological approaches that we believe have the potential to disrupt traditional research models. We begin by explaining the term and tracing its conceptualization across academic disciplines and popular culture. In conversation with this literature, we then propose four broad contours that guide rasquache methodologies, explaining how each contour might subvert, resist, refract, and perhaps even purposefully exaggerate Eurocentric standards. We move to situate these contours within our shared rasquache research and close by emphasizing the potential and future directions of rasquache methodologies.

What Is Rasquache?

Simply put, rasquache/rasquachismx means making the most with the everyday tools one has. As Chicano scholar Tomas Ybarra-Frausto (1989) writes, "rasquachismo is . . . deployed in immediate, day-to-day living . . . [and] springs from making do with what's at hand (hacer rendir las cosas)" (p. 5). An ingenuity born from a perpetual insistence to survive the daily grind of society's structured inequalities with dignity, rasquache is a material descriptor (a rasquache house, garden, car) and an action (rasquache *comportamientos*, movidas, etc.) (Mendoza Aviña & Morales, 2022; Ybarra-Frausto, 1991). Hence, one might call a reused butter container "rasquache Tupperware" while teasing the user for being rasquache.

Historically, though, rasquache has not always been seen in a positive light. Rasquache was a word or phrase used to describe something tacky, vulgar, and unruly, particularly associated with so-called low-class forms of working-class Mexican and Mexican-descended people (Mirandé, 2011). However, with the rise of the 1960s Chicana/o/x Movement, Chicanxs[1] reappropriated the term as a symbol of pride and resistance. As a joyfully defiant response to colonial knowledge systems, Chicanxs' flipping of a derogatory term (*rasquache*) validated ancestral ways of knowing that stem from making do with what is available. In this vein, rasquachismx symbolizes the resilience of Chicanx communities in disrupting oppressive forces by using whatever resources they have to recreate and remix theory, knowledge, and art (Gaspar de Alba, 1998).

Foundational Texts and Important Theorists

The foundational essay *Rasquachismo: A Chicano Sensibility* was published in 1989 by Chicano Art and Humanities scholar Thomas Ybarra-Frausto, establishing raquachismx as a significant concept in both academic and popular culture. In this essay, he describes the working-class subtleties of Chicanx art, defining rasquachismx as "a sensibility that is not elevated and serious, but playful and elemental" (p. 8).[2] He explained that Chicanx art is rooted in an aesthetic of resourcefulness and creativity, in which Chicanxs engage in a practice of transforming something out of nothing. In other words, rasquachismo involves taking what might be considered tacky and useless (e.g., an old, discarded car) and transforming it into something that is valuable (e.g., the lowrider).

Building on Ybarra-Frausto's work, other Chicanx and Latinx studies scholars have worked to make conceptualizations of rasquache more inclusive and intersectional. For example, artist Amalia Mesa-Bains (1999) agrees that rasquache is grounded in resourceful, if not excessive, inventiveness and resilience, but she also advances a view rooted in feminist theory. In her groundbreaking essay, *Domesticana: The Sensibility of Chicana Rasquache*, Mesa-Bains (1999) examines sacred home spaces, in particular the accumulative, bric-a-brac-ish, and often healing properties of altars and shrines, as feminine rasquache movidas. She writes that *domesticana*, an extension of rasquachismx, is useful for describing her and other Chicana artists' efforts to undo "the wounds of patriarchy and colonization" (p. 166). In a similar vein, Diaz (2017) argues how queerness and rasquachismo are not mutually exclusive, and as such, scholars can highlight queer(er) iterations, articulations, and futures of rasquache aesthetics, subjectivities, and movidas. Finally, Mendoza Aviña (2016), Mendoza Aviña and Morales (2022), and Gonzales (2022) ask researchers and activists to critically assess the opportunities and limitations of comparing adjacent racial and cultural expressions like ratchet, a Black feminine rejection of respectability.

Education scholars, too, have begun to survey the pedagogical and curricular possibilities of rasquache/rasquachismx. For instance, Morales and colleagues (2016) explore the development of rasquache pedagogy as a healing praxis in ethnic studies courses. This work highlights the classroom as an adaptive collection of humanizing practices in which students and teachers of color benefit from loving, spontaneous, and "as-needed" movidas. In conversation with this work, Mendoza Aviña (2016) introduces a Chicana feminist rasquache pedagogy which "centers on and reflects the everyday realities of Latinx youth, recognizing their forms of survival and resistance, as well as their embodied knowledges and daily practices as valuable pedagogical formations" (p. 468). Her work provides an important perspective on how educators can adopt a rasquache pedagogy to support Latinx youth. Lastly, Monreal (2021) attends to rasquachismx by illuminating Latinx teachers' movidas of rasquache. By showcasing Latinx teachers' engagement in rasquache practices, Monreal reveals that teachers "create spaces of counter-conduct where educators struggle toward new subjectivities" (p. 37). Overall, the scholarly contributions within the field of education offer a new perspective for applying rasquache/rasquachismx within education settings. However, conceptualizations of rasquache (as) methodology remain underexplored.

What Is Rasquache/Rasquachismx (as) Methodology?

We position rasquache as a cross-disciplinary methodology rooted in Meso-American and working-class knowledge systems and practices. Inherently malleable and porous, and not representative of all Chicanx and/or Latinx people, we root ideas of rasquache methodologies in both the inventive, "find-a-way" sensibilities of researchers *and* their complementary scrappy movidas (see Espinoza et al., 2018). While we consider the disposition and doing of rasquache methodologies as two sides of the same coin, we share examples of each before moving toward four general contours.

A rasquache stance continually (re)imagines the utility and beauty of life's mundane scraps, transforming the ordinary into the *extra*-ordinary (Rao, 2023).[3] A rasquache perspective is significant in the research design because it asserts the necessity to center those people, places, challenges, and successes that mainstream research(ers) often dismiss. An illustration of this is Mejia and Pulido's (2018) study, which examines how Latinx youth develop engineering skills through their involvement in family businesses. In highlighting the soldering, tinkering, and repurposing of things like recipes, ovens, and materials, we see the funds of knowledge, design thinking, trial and error, and cost-benefit analysis that evidence substantial scientific thinking. Another mode of rasquache thinking is what researchers count, combine, and create as theory, literature, and context for a research study. Leading up to his dissertation (Monreal, 2020), Tim used a rasquache lens to pull together a literature review that included traditional academic literature and newspapers, podcasts, conference presentations, conversations, and (traditional, social, and online) media. Hence, moving toward rasquache methodologies is an epistemological move to value creative ingenuity in the process of knowledge production.

A rasquache methodology is also what researchers do, a praxis that is not beholden to established and extractive methods. Just as Abuelita might repurpose leftover tile and glass to create a *maceta*, a rasquache approach blends various, sometimes mismatched, methods to answer novel research questions. Hidalgo's (2015) creation of augmented fotonovelas, using methodological tools from Chicanx Studies, Education, Visual Anthropology, and Geography, exemplifies this. Her process of "digital rasquachismo" involved using cost-effective technologies and community resourcefulness to repurpose and reinvent tools for creative improvisation that addressed community needs (p. 303). Similarly, the two of us (Patrón-Vargas & Monreal, under review) combined autoethnography, pláticas, letter-writing, and photovoice to explore how rasquachismx supports university faculty members. As we discuss near the end of this chapter, combining various methods not only helped us make sense of our experiences but also emphasized a level of joy and creativity that academic life often jettisons.

In sum, we ground our conceptualizations of rasquache methodologies in the various ways that everyday Chicanxs/Latinxs have historically used whatever resources are available to create new meaning (Patrón-Vargas & Monreal, under review), a worldview and praxis perfectly in line with the charge of university and community researchers. A rasquache methodology presents an innovative approach to meaning-making by challenging researchers to use their critical social imagination, embrace their embodied experiences, and tap into resourcefulness. Below, we sketch four broad contours that guide rasquache methodologies.

Contour 1: Chicana/Latina Feminisms

Rasquache methodologies are guided by Chicanx/Latinx knowledge systems and practices. Specifically, we ground rasquache methodologies in Chicana/Latina feminisms. Driven by Chicana/Latina feminisms (e.g., Anzaldúa, 1989; Delgado Bernal, 2001; Mesa-Bains, 1999), rasquache methodologies in education aim to unveil the movidas, including "the strategic and tactical but also the undercover, the dissident, the illicit—that which is not part of approved and publicly acknowledged political strategies, histories, and economic and social relations" (Espinoza et al., 2018, p. 2). Importantly, there is a deep interconnection between method and epistemology, as the informal ways we make sense of the world—pláticas, palabras, kitchen tables, chisme, consejos, dance, and art—are refashioned as formal research methods. Hence, rasquachismo challenges dominant knowledge systems by positioning the embodied experiences and practices of Chicanxs/Latinxs communities as valuable sites for shared knowledge creation.

Contour 2: Co-constructing Knowledge

Rasquachismo stands on the belief that students, elders, researchers—all participants, including *los de abajo*—are creators and holders of knowledge (Delgado Bernal, 2001). In doing so, it views the creation of knowledge as emerging through our relationships with participants, ancestors, and the world around us. Rasquache methodologies, then, honor the *process* of producing truth(s) in/with community rather than a quest to discover and represent a truth (Monreal & Tirado, 2023). This departs from dominant models of research that position the researcher as objective and the findings as a representation of one objective reality. Rasquache, like other Chicanx/Latinx methodologies, begins with the premise that both the researcher and participants are active participants in the conversation. Through this reciprocal exchange, all participants have the opportunity to share, co-create knowledge, and be vulnerable in the process.

Contour 3: The Art of Creative Resourcefulness

Rasquache methodologies call for research methods that mirror our communities' DIY, proudly *chingón* creativities. Rooted in improvisation and resourcefulness, rasquache methodologies embrace the beauty of contradiction, tension, and messiness, of using our low-class upbringings to redefine and resist the higher-class spaces of research. Unlike mainstream paradigms of research, which often view the research process as linear, static, and transactional, rasquache methodologies require a critical and imaginative engagement with the research process. As such, rasquache methodology invites researchers and participants to theorize from the "messiness" (dare we say the *mierda*) of fragmented odds and ends, leaning into and finding humor in the productive possibilities that emerge from life in flux (see also Monreal and Tirado, 2023; Monreal et al., 2024).

Contour 4: Joy, Humor, and Serious Play

The work of a rasquache researcher is a tremendous and humbling honor, playing a fundamental role in advocating for change, recentering our communities, and reimagining educational spaces. It is also a joyful praxis. Our own processes of sharing childhood photos, stories, and traditions were affirming and healing. We have found that the practice of turning what is seen as shameful into something meaningful offers deep insight and joy. Monreal et al. (2024) name this idea "unserious seriousness and playful insubordination" (p. 218). Similarly, we hold it is possible to demand dignity with humor and (lack of) style to "outsmart adversity by wit, wile, and street smarts" (p. 218). Thus, rasquache foregrounds natural inquisitiveness, reclaiming the natural curiosity that dominant schooling and academic preparation seek to stifle.

How Rasquache Methodologies Are Used in Our Research

The inspiration for engaging rasquache methodologies came from a desire to challenge Eurocentric research standards. Trained in conventional research methods, we both felt conflicted using methods that did not necessarily align with or mirror our epistemological positionings. As critical scholars, these tensions pushed us to analyze our own methodological training and seek other methodologies that better represent the communities we seek to serve. In what follows, we provide a snapshot of how we have used rasquache methodologies in our research.

Growing up, rasquache was integral to our daily lives, influencing everything from the aesthetic choices in our homes to movidas to challenge capitalist influences. In our collaborative research (see Patrón-Vargas & Monreal, under review), we combined autoethnography, pláticas, letter-writing, and photovoice to explore how rasquachismx is a tool for surviving and thriving as university faculty members. Our process began with a deep dive into our own histories, revisiting how rasquache became woven into our lives. We held virtual pláticas, informal conversations, in which we shared photos and stories of our rasquache upbringings (Delgado Bernal et al., 2023). These sessions became a cache of joy and laughter, filled with stories of how our families turned discarded items into creative wonders. For example, Tim recounted how his family reworked second-hand items to create a makeshift garage. As we engaged in reflexivity, we uncovered parallels between our family's rasquache ingenuity and our journeys through and beyond academia. In this way, rasquache methodologies affirm the material realities and ancestral wisdom of Chicanx/Latinx communities, anchoring the research in ordinary lived experiences.

Conducting research grounded in our material realities and familial practices also prompted us to rethink the process of data generation and analysis. As we considered how to collect and analyze, we embraced the improvisational nature of rasquachismx, allowing the data to guide us in unexpected directions. This meant casting aside the notion of the researcher as the expert and entering a space of liminality (Anzaldúa, 1989). For example, instead of following a step-by-step procedure, we fluctuated between historias, fotos, notas, and analysis because we came to the consensus that these stages are perpetually in flux. This is a departure from Eurocentric models that attempt to compartmentalize and predefine the research process. Thus, adopting rasquache methodologies pushes researchers and participants to embody its improvisational principles, creating a collaborative and fluid research environment.

As our discussion progressed, we met to narrow the themes emerging from our virtual exchanges and shared media. As we began theorizing the role of rasquachismx in and outside of the academy, we found ourselves frequently sharing memes and other media, realizing that these were not just peripheral but central to our "data analysis" process. For instance, during our analysis, we drew from various sources, including academic literature, memes, television shows, and personal reflections. Much like the inventive ways our families repurposed items, we, too, remixed diverse sources to make sense of our data. Therefore, for researchers to engage this methodological approach, they must engage a creative process in which both academic literature and everyday materials serve as valuable tools for interpreting and understanding data.

Conclusion

An artful blend of ingenuity, resourcefulness, and Chicanx/Latinx ways of knowing, rasquache methodology unlocks a gateway to critical imagination. As a methodology, rasquache encourages both researchers and participants to recreate, remix, and upcycle materials, ideas, and approaches—put simply, to use *nuestros recursos*, or what we have at our disposal, such as memes saved in our digital archive, to explore methods for new meaning. In this chapter, we offer four broad contours of rasquache methodologies. Neither prescriptive nor descriptive, these serve as a starting point for the evolution of rasquache methodologies.

Ultimately, rasquache (as) methodology challenges us to reconsider how we engage with and interpret the world. Through our examination, we illustrate how rasquache methodologies subvert conventional standards by emphasizing the value of messiness and spontaneity inherent in lived experiences and everyday creativity. Moreover, this approach's iterative and improvisational nature allows for a more fluid and responsive research process that draws upon the full spectrum of *nuestros recursos* to create multifaceted and vibrantly dynamic knowledge. By engaging with rasquache, researchers can then forge new approaches to better understand the complexities of Chicanxs/Latinxs and other working-class communities. As we continue to explore what rasquache methodologies might offer us, we open the door to research practices that are fluid and innovative and that consider how ordinary acts (of defiance) offer us profound insights.

Notes

1. We use the terms *Chicanx*, *Latinx*, and *rasquachismx* to promote inclusivity and visibility of gender nonconforming people.

2. Comically, Ybarra-Frausto (1991) uses words from a Chicano theater performer to write, "rasquachismo is when you use a loaf of bread as a prop, and somebody eats it" (p. 160).

3. We italicize extra to show the many ways a rasquache stance adds meaning to the word. As just two examples, one can be "*extra*" in the sense of adding flair, personality, and exaggeration just as something can become extraordinary by adding value and significance.

Suggestions for Further Reading and References

Anzaldúa, G. (1989). *Borderlands/La Frontera: The new mestiza.* Aunt Lute Books.

Delgado Bernal, D. (2001). Learning and living pedagogies of the home: The mestiza consciousness of Chicana students. *International Journal of Qualitative Studies in Education, 14*(5), 623–639. https://doi.org/10.1080/09518390110059838

Delgado Bernal, D., Flores, A. I., Gaxiola Serrano, T. J., & Morales, S. (2023). An introduction: Chicana/Latina feminista pláticas in educational research. *International Journal of Qualitative Studies in Education, 36*(9), 1627–1630. https://doi.org/10.1080/09518398.2023.2203113

Diaz, E. M. (2017). A genealogy of rasquache and camp: Luis Alfaro and the Royal Chicano Air Force. *ASAP/Journal, 2*(1), 105–129.

Espinoza, D., Cotera, M. E., & Blackwell, M. (Eds.). (2018). *Chicana movidas: New narratives of activism and feminism in the movement era* (First edition). University of Texas Press.

Gaspar de Alba, A. (1998). Born in East L.A.: An exercise in cultural schizophrenia. In R. Delgado & J. Stefancic, *The Latina/o Condition: A Critical Reader* (1st ed.). New York University Press.

Gonzales, T. I. (2022). Ratchet-Rasquache activism: Aesthetic and discursive frames within Chicago-based women-of-color activism. *Social Problems, 69*(2), 380–397. https://doi.org/10.1093/socpro/spaa034

Hidalgo, L. (2015). Augmented fotonovelas: Creating new media as pedagogical and social Justice tools. *Qualitative Inquiry, 21*(3), 300–314. https://doi.org/10.1177/1077800414557831

Medina-López, K. (2017). Rasquache rhetorics: A cultural rhetorics sensibility. *Constellations, May*, 1–23.

Mejia, J. A., & Pulido, A. L. (2018). *Fregados pero no jodidos: A case study of Latinx rasquachismo.* Paper Presentation. American Society for Engineering Education, Salt Lake City, UT.

Mendoza Aviña, S. (2016). "That's ratchet": A Chicana feminist rasquache pedagogy as entryway to understanding the material realities of contemporary Latinx elementary-aged youth. *Equity & Excellence in Education, 49*(4), 468–479. https://doi.org/10.1080/10665684.2016.1227158

Mendoza Aviña, S., & Morales, S. (2022). Towards a rasquache resistance: Conceptualizing Chicanx youth subjectivities. *Urban Education, 59*(7), 2096–2123. 004208592210929. https://doi.org/10.1177/00420859221092974

Mesa-Bains, A. (1999). "Domesticana": The sensibility of Chicana rasquache. *Aztlán: A Journal of Chicano Studies, 24*(2), 157–167.

Mirandé, A. (2011). *Rascuache lawyer: Toward a theory of ordinary litigation*. University of Arizona Press.

Monreal, T. (2020). *Hecho en South Carolina: K-12 Latinx educators made in, and remaking, El Sur Latinx* [Dissertation]. University of South Carolina.

Monreal, T. (2021). Stitching together more expansive Latinx teacher self/ves: Movidas of rasquache and spaces of counter-conduct in El Sur Latinx. *Theory, Research, and Action in Urban Education, 6*(1), 37–51.

Monreal, T., & Tirado, J. (2023). The (self/re)generating sacred energy called Teotl: Using Nahua philosophy to introduce posthumanist thinking. In B. A. Varga, T. Monreal, & R. C. Christ (Eds.), *Toward a stranger and more posthuman social studies* (pp. 139–148). Teachers College Press.

Monreal, T., Tirado, J., & Barrera, S. (2024). Rasquache movidas toward critical, intersectional Latinx futures in the social studies. In A. T. Jaffee & C. Salinas (Eds.), *Teaching culturally and linguistically relevant social studies for emergent bilingual and multilingual youth*. Teachers College Press.

Morales, S., Aviña, S., & Delgado Bernal, D. (2016). Education in Nepantla: A Chicana feminist approach to engaging Latina/o elementary youth in ethnic studies. In D. M. Sandoval, A. J. Ratcliff, T. L. Buenavista, & J. R. Marín (Eds.), *"White" washing American education: The new culture wars in ethnic studies [volume 1]* (pp. 67–93). Praegar.

Rao, A. (2023). On the home front, a Latine aesthetic's ordinary exuberance. *Untapped, 4*. https://www.untappedjournal.com/issues/issue-4/rasquachismo-architecture-home-ordinary-exuberance

Ybarra-Frausto, T. (1989). *Rasquachismo: A Chicano sensibility*. Artspace.

Ybarra-Frausto, T. (1991). Rasquachismo: A Chicano sensibility. In R. Griswold Del Castillo, T. McKenna, & Yarbro-Bejarano (Eds.), *Chicano art: Resistance and affirmation, 1965-1985* (pp. 155–162). Wright Art Gallery, UCLA.

Chapter 3 Discussion Questions

1. How do rasquache methodologies challenge dominant Eurocentric epistemologies in research? Reflect on how these methodologies might redefine knowledge production.
2. The authors emphasize the importance of resourcefulness and improvisation in rasquache methodologies. How might adopting these principles influence the research process in your field? Can you identify examples from your own academic or personal experiences where resourcefulness shaped an outcome?
3. Drawing on the discussion of Chicana/Latina feminisms and queerness in the chapter, how do rasquache methodologies incorporate and expand upon intersectional approaches? What are the implications for addressing systemic inequalities in research?
4. The chapter describes messiness and spontaneity as central to rasquache methodologies. Discuss how embracing messiness might offer opportunities in educational research. How could this perspective be applied to disrupt traditional methods in your current or future research projects?

FOUR

All the World's A Stage: Ethnodrama as Critical Qualitative Research

John H. Samuels

What is Ethnodrama?

IN *METHOD MEETS ART: ARTS-BASED Research Practice*, Patricia Leavy (2020) details the synergistic energies of the arts and qualitative research writing. Leavy shows us that qualitative research, like artistic work, is about (re)presenting meanings to an audience. Both aim to illuminate, build understanding or challenge assumptions, reveal aspects of the social world, portray people sensitively, develop new sociohistorical insights, and/or disrupt dominant narratives. In short, Leavy argues that the arts offer researchers a broad range of tools to investigate and communicate social meanings.

Ethnodrama, an arts-based method, can be a powerful disruptive vehicle for qualitative researchers. *Ethnodrama* is a combination of ethnography and drama, where a written play script is created from ethnographic or autoethnographic data collection. Saldaña (2016) stated that the goal of ethnodrama is "to investigate a particular facet of the human condition for purposes of adapting those observations and insights into a performance medium" (pp. 12–13). Plays have long been used to capture the human experience in cathartic ways, and the artistic capabilities of drama can be leveraged to document and present findings and insights on lived realities (Saldaña, 2016).

Anyone can write an ethnodrama; however, those who choose this method need to have some understanding of both qualitative research and drama. This understanding can come from reading plays or attending playwriting workshops and classes. Joe Salvatore (2018; 2020) urges researchers to seek training in areas including playwriting, script development, and dramaturgy so that the performative and aesthetic integrity of the work is upheld. Saldaña (2016) shares similar sentiments, stressing the importance of ensuring that ethnodramatic researchers are aware of the "socially conscious merit and artistic quality" (p. 32) that should live in the work. Without this attention to detail, ethnodramatic studies can fall short of their intended purpose. While the training does not have to be formal, there should be a level of commitment to the medium of drama.

The process and construction of an ethnodrama are unique to each individual and largely depend on the researcher, the study, and the data (Salvatore, 2018). However, scripts are traditionally created from qualitative data sets that include but are not limited to: interview transcripts, field notes, journal entries, personal memories, and personal correspondence. Before any data is collected and throughout the ethnodramatic research process, it is important to inform and remind the participants that this work will be dramatized and share the performance goals of the project, as it could be jarring to read their lived experience in an artistic and embodied way (Saldaña, 2016). When interviewing participants, Salvatore (2018; 2020) relies on open-ended prompts to help encourage participants to share their experiences. He also utilizes a Participant Characteristics and Physical Surroundings Survey when reviewing field notes that contain helpful information for researchers, actors, costume designers, or scenic designers as they portray and design the performance based on the data.

When transcribing interviews, scholars such as Salvatore and Anna Deavere Smith (2001) refrain from traditional qualitative interview transcription methods that delete or alter nuances of the language, like pauses, stumbles, and other changes in cadence. These researchers embrace the meaning-making and possibilities that emerge when language breaks down. By attending to pauses, stumbles, and shifts in cadence during interview transcriptions, ethnodramatists can uncover additional layers of insight into both the content and delivery of participants' narratives. This is especially true when scripts remain close to the verbatim language of participants, adding depth and complexity to the analysis. The coding process for ethnodrama is highly adaptable and shaped by the project's specific needs, goals, and aesthetic vision. One effective approach is dramaturgical coding, as outlined by Saldaña (2021). This method involves categorizing data into six key components of character analysis: objectives, conflicts/obstacles, tactics/strategies, attitudes, emotions, and subtexts. By systematically reflecting on and organizing data within these categories, researchers can uncover connections among the codes. These insights serve as a foundation for developing characters, storylines, and motives, ultimately guiding the creation of a cohesive and compelling script.

Once coding is complete, prevalent themes are identified, and the research team determines what essential information must be included, again keeping in mind what is needed both scientifically and artistically (Taylor et al., 2017). Scripts go through multiple revisions throughout the research process, with many scholars using strategies such as triangulation, member checks, and read-throughs of the scripts. These strategies help ensure accuracy, strengthen dramatic elements, include more perspective, and add depth to the performance text (Saldaña, 2016; Salvatore, 2020).

Disrupting Systems of Oppression and Empowering Participants

"But when it comes to ethnodrama, there is one principle I've learned the hard way and now always try to hold onto: participants first, playwrights second, and audiences third" (Saldaña, 2016, pp. 42–43). Saldaña reminds researchers that the most important part of ethnodramatic research is how the participants want to be represented in the script. If one is not mindful, qualitative research can be driven by the interests and priorities of the researcher, with research being performed *on* participants instead of *with* them. With this approach, participants would not have a voice in the study's execution and might not share its values. Ethnodramas can put the participant in the *driver's seat* of the research by giving them an active role in the construction of the work. Through constant collaboration throughout the composition of the script, the participant is part of the research team to honor their lives and ethically create a play that preserves the aesthetics and research of the project. To do this, Vachon et al. (2019) spend significant time before and while working on the script to make sure there is clarity in the research purpose of the project and to understand how the research team's life experiences relate to the communities of participants in the ethnodrama. For scholar artists like Saldaña (2016), giving participants a copy of all play drafts throughout the writing of the script provides an opportunity for participants to give feedback on the accuracy of the script and give feedback on their representation in the work.

Scholar-artist Joe Salvatore (2018; 2020) understands how jarring it can be to not only experience oneself portrayed in traditional research but also the discomfort that may arise through the artistic representation of their experience. The collaborative process between Salvatore and participants includes an honest presentation of his research process and providing the opportunity for participants to request that parts of the interview not be included in the ethnodrama. If he notices any hesitancies or discomfort in the overall interview experience, he will not consider the interview in the coding process to ensure that he does not "offend, retraumatize, or endanger an individual participating in the research process" (Salvatore, 2020, p. 1048). With a strict obligation to the participant first, ethnodrama as a method can help to better engage participants in the research.

Academic research can be verbose and full of discipline-specific language and jargon. For thousands of years, plays have been used to document and share the human experience in modern language, and relying on plays in research can provide participants, audiences, and the broader community with a level of understanding through everyday language that may not be achieved through more traditional research.

Incorporating the dramatic arts into research presents participatory opportunities for the communities in which the work is situated and for broader audiences. Ethnodramas lend themselves to talkbacks or a reading of the script with a facilitated post-show discussion. Talkbacks provide participants, the audience, and the community with a chance to share observations, feedback, reflections, and moments of ambiguity or confusion. Using these comments, the playwright/researcher can make the necessary adjustments that can sharpen the rigor, message, research, and aesthetics of the work (Kanter, 2015; Urbinati, 2016). Talkbacks allow for direct involvement in the script development process (Urbinati, 2016), potentially minimizing the top-down hierarchical structure of research and granting access and power to the participants and the community.

Foundational Texts and Important Theorists

The dramatic arts have a long history of advancing and disseminating knowledge and research long before they gained traction as a distinct line of inquiry in the late 20th century when social science research explored new ways of presenting findings and recognized the value of dramatic performance as both method and dissemination.

In the late 1940s and early 1950s, psychiatrist and social scientist Dr. Jacob L. Moreno developed psychodrama and sociodrama as a form of psychotherapy (1946). Using drama and theater as a means of therapy, Moreno used these methods to help participants explore past situations, inner mental processes, social events, and collective ideologies. Moreno published duplications of his sessions to help the field better understand the experience and communicate his methods and discoveries.

Norman K. Denzin's (2018) work explored the use of performance to conduct and present ethnographic research. He explained how, through performance methods such as ethnodrama, the researcher has an immediate and emotional engagement with participants and viewers by positioning them as active participants in social transformation. Denzin (2018) stated, "This performance ethic asks that interpretive work provide the foundations for social criticism by subjecting specific programs and policies to concrete analysis. Performers show how specific policies and practices affect and effect their lives" (p. 66). Denzin called for the disruption of traditional qualitative methods and approaches through researchers tapping into the performative, reflexive, and critical power of performance—transforming researchers into playwrights, performers, and storytellers.

Johnny Saldaña has significant contributions that have helped advance ethnodrama as method and inquiry (2005; 2016). In his work, Saldaña shares guidelines, processes, suggestions, and examples of turning ethnographic data into performance scripts and performances. He makes an important distinction between the ethnodramatic script and the theatrical production of the script. Saldaña (2016) calls the theatrical production of the script *ethnotheatre*, combining the words ethnography and theater to perform the stories of the participants and the researcher's interpretations of the data. Bringing his theater training and practice to qualitative research, Saldaña provides rich background information, context, and theoretical analyses on the art of merging the dramatic arts and qualitative research.

These contributions highlight a shift in research that leverages the dramatic, performative, and artistic talents of both researchers and the participants they collaborate with. Saldaña (2016) asserts that ethnodramas should "progressively advance [their] source participants, creators, body of dramatic literature, readers, audiences, and the broader communities they involve, to new and richer domains of social and artistic meaning" (p. 32). Emphasizing both the social and the artistic can use the power of drama to shed light on human experiences and promote social change.

Suggestions for Further Reading and References

Cannon, A. (2012). Making the data perform: An ethnodramatic analysis. *Qualitative Inquiry, 18*(7), 583–594. https://doi.org/10.1177/1077800412450153

Denzin, N. K. (2018). *Performance autoethnography: Critical pedagogy and the politics of culture* (Second edition.). Routledge. https://doi.org/10.4324/9781315159270

Kanter, J. (2015). *Talkbacks: Asking good discussion questions* (pp. 518–523). Routledge. https://doi.org/10.4324/9780203075944-95

Leavy, P. (2020). *Method meets art: Arts-based research practice* (Third edition.). The Guilford Press.

Moreno, J. L., & Moreno, Z. T. (1946). *Psychodrama* (Volume 1.). Beacon House.

Saldaña, J. (2005). *Ethnodrama: An anthology of reality theatre.* AltaMira Press.

Saldaña, J. (2016). *Ethnotheatre: Research from page to stage.* Routledge.

Saldaña, J. (2021). *The coding manual for qualitative researchers* (Fourth edition.). SAGE Publications.

Salvatore, J. (2018). Ethnodrama and ethnotheatre. In P. Leavy (Ed.), *Handbook of arts-based research* (pp. 267–287). The Guilford Press.

Salvatore, J. (2020). Scripting the Ethnodrama. In P. Leavy (Ed.), *The Oxford Handbook of Qualitative Research* (2nd ed.). Oxford University Press. https://doi.org/10.1093/oxfordhb/9780190847388.013.5

Smith, A. Deavere. (2001). *Talk to me: Travels in media and politics* (1st Anchor Books ed.). Anchor Books.

Taylor, J., Namey, E., Carrington Johnson, A., & Guest, G. (2017). Beyond the page: A process review of using ethnodrama to disseminate research findings. *Journal of Health Communication, 22*(6), 532–544. https://doi.org/10.1080/10810730.2017.1317303

Urbinati, R. (2016). *Audiences and Talkbacks* (1st ed., pp. 179–185). Focal Press. https://doi.org/10.4324/9781315732329-16

Vachon, W., Hossain, R., Ramsay, N., Moore, M., & Milo, M. (2019). Frictions and actions: The actor's role in ethnodrama. *Qualitative Inquiry, 25*(2), 118–129. https://doi.org/10.1177/1077800417746424

Chapter 4 Discussion Questions

1. Discuss the importance of prioritizing participants' voices and representations in ethnodramatic research. How do strategies such as participant collaboration and feedback on scripts contribute to ethical research practices?
2. Ethnodrama combines the rigor of qualitative research with the creativity of drama. How can researchers balance scientific accuracy with artistic quality when creating ethnodramas? What challenges might arise, and how can they be addressed?
3. Ethnodrama offers participatory opportunities through talkbacks and collaborative processes. How might these practices challenge traditional hierarchies in research and empower participants and communities? Provide examples of how these practices can create a more inclusive research process.
4. Denzin (2018) emphasized the transformative potential of performance in ethnography. How can ethnodramatic performances serve as tools for social criticism and change? Discuss examples of how a performance might highlight systemic issues or empower marginalized communities.

FIVE

Sonic Interruptions: Centering Listening in Qualitative Research

Walter S. Gershon and Boni Wozolek

Despite continuing and increasing sonic attention in qualitative research, most of its expressions—from academic papers to theater and from Arts Based Research to narrative forms—are ocular (e.g., Cahnmann-Taylor & Siegesmund, 2017; Leavy, 2020). From a Western five-senses perspective, there is only one sense where more than human animals can falsely believe they are the epicenter of anything: sight. Our point is not that seeing things is necessarily problematic or that metaphors are necessarily always harmful. Rather, it is our position that a metaphoric overreliance on the ocular creates relational and literal myopia in qualitative research and educational ecologies (Gershon 2011, 2017, forthcoming; Wozolek, 2018, 2019, 2023).

In qualitative research, the ocular, from a researcher's gaze to textual presentations of another's life, is in many ways the cornerstone of essentializing, extractive practices that are forms of colonization (Bhattacharya, 2009; Smith, 1999/2021). It is not lost on us that questions of relationality, care, education, and justice focus on auralities and forms of listening for many, if not most, Indigenous Wisdom Traditions (Brearley, 2015; Knight, 2021; Robinson, 2020).

It is also important to note that the sonic is by no means neutral—as harmful as helpful, attenuating as much as amplifying—and its application to one's argument or broader understandings ultimately expresses more than human animals' sonic biases for speaker and listener alike. However, unlike sight, sounds can neither be framed nor binary, and the sonic makes its directionality (Gershon, forthcoming) clear: from the outside to the listener, even if you're listening to yourself.

These are especially significant questions about educational ecologies in general and schooling in specific. As we have documented in our continuing work—both independently (e.g., Gershon, 2017; Wozolek, 2023) and together (e.g., Wozolek & Gershon, 2024)—education is a painfully sighted affair where sonic questions are most often unidirectional critiques from teachers about their observations of student behaviors. Sounds are also generally punitive, stemming from antiquated notions about the value of quietude that are, in turn, contemporary expressions of class, race, gender, and the like (Lei, 2003; Morris, 2016). Think, for example, of how "good" behavior in a classroom is often linked to expectations of silence unless called upon by the teacher. As Morris (2016) and others have explored, expressions of joy and community norms, such as laughter and other exchanges, are considered disruptive to classroom productivity and whitestream (Urrieta, 2009) norms in schools.

Our understandings of sonic attentions within qualitative research, and the shoulders on which we stand, bring us to the following critical, educational questions: Will you listen to others? Can you hear without having something to watch? What does it mean that you'll read for a few hours straight but can't listen to a 10-minute sound composition about young people's lives? What does this say about us as educators? What does it mean that listening in school is more about power relations in taxonomic hierarchies than about care, dignity, or justice?

This chapter advances an argument that listening is the key to strong, ethical work in qualitative research, education, and educational qualitative research. We have previously advanced aspects of this argument while continuing to explore possibilities for the sonic across areas of study, cultivating material practices and their associated ideas and ideals within qualitative research and educational studies. As an extension of this discussion, we have again come together to provide a more concise, declarative discussion on the significance of listening. We present this argument for at least the following three important reasons.

First, despite decades of scholarship to the contrary, qualitative studies in education remain solidly grounded in the ocular. At a moment when there are increasing claims of decolonial qualitative methodologies and calls for decolonizing curricula and pedagogies, it is worth attending to continual reliance on the very ocular tendencies that are foundational to extractive colonial practices. To be clear, this is not a claim that attention to sonic understandings is somehow better than other research tools and their associated methodologies or that sonically oriented research cannot be colonizing. Rather, this is an argument that considers how the senses are increasingly discussed in contemporary Western cultures and, relatedly, research, but that the sonic remains generally overlooked against what many consider to be evidence-based ways of being, knowing, and doing, rooted in the ocular.

Second, it continues to be the case that no small amount of scholarship in educational qualitative research contains a central irony: that well-documented arguments are somehow novel. Such presentations of novelty are possible only if one does not listen to either the history of educational scholarship or holds fast to a hubris of expertise that conflates a lack of awareness with a dearth of scholarship. Further, to overlook histories is, in itself, an act of colonization, in that it claims a space as its own, ignoring well-established histories in order to gain capital.

Third, and perhaps most importantly, qualitative research that prioritizes listening as a performative act serves to explicitly articulate the researcher's ethical commitments to their collaborators and the communities. For instance, traditional frameworks such as member checks, participatory research, arts-based practices, and decolonial methodologies emphasize an "outward-in" directionality. This approach involves critically listening to and engaging with the broader ecological contexts. This is a kind of critical listening to associated ecologies, from communities to cities (e.g., Plourde, 2019) to forests (e.g., Kohn, 2013).

In keeping with the aim and scope of this volume, we turn our attentions to the sonic attunements that drive our research projects, associated scholarship, and everyday pedagogical practices. As scholars who understand ourselves as nodes in continuing sonic studies within and outside of education, we situate our experiences and understandings so that they both a) amplify such complex sets of inter/intra/relations and b) articulate what embodied, material listening can mean and do for qualitative research in education. Toward these ends, this paper will first engage with what it means to be listening, documenting the significance of this across qualitative research methodologies and, specifically, educational contexts. Next, we turn to the historical underpinnings that inform our work, followed by a brief concluding section.

Why Listening Is Central to All Qualitative Research

Forms of listening are literally, metaphorically, and relationally central to any and all qualitative research processes. This is because the notion of listening, of being aware and attuned to ecologies and relations, is what qualitative researchers do. Although this framing may seem a bit grandiose, consider what it is that we, as qualitative researchers, do—from how we conceptualize research processes to the practical, material ways such processes unfold. As we argue in this section, while it is the ocular that gets our attention in qualitative methodologies, even the "multi" in "multimodality" in education comes from a literacy group (Bearne & Wolstencroft, 2007; Eisner, 1991) and essentially means "not only text," our ethical commitments and focus are questions of listening.

Metaphorically, notions of listening are how we often describe paying attention to information that flows to us from outside ourselves. It is the case that thinking about qualitative research in terms of metaphor can be understood as a leftover postmodernism, a tendency to anthropomorphize and universalize interactions and relations (Carpenter, 2008). However, we mean *metaphorically* in a larger critical fashion. From our perspective, entanglements or assemblages are metaphors for the never-ending imbricated enmeshment of things and their relations. Or, from a more everyday expression of these understandings, a young person's or teen's "*cry* for help" is often a sociobehavioral change that we *hear* as a need for a particular kind of care and attention.

Listening also resides at the center of our ethical commitments (Noblit, 1999) as researchers and, for that matter, as educators. It is not an accident that many forms of qualitative research that seek to work in more ethical trajectories towards possibilities for justice and liberation tend to focus on questions of listening (e.g., McKittrick, 2020; Robinson, 2020; Weheliye, 2023). We work to listen to our research collaborators, those with whom we work when we do qualitative research. In these processes, we work with our collaborators to ensure how we voice our distillation of events and subsequent understandings, echo their intentions to amplify the significance of their ways of *beingknowingdoing*. As such, we are aligned with Wolcott (1990) when he expressed a deep desire not to get it all wrong as we work toward foregrounding collaborators' dignity in our work. This is a deep, careful listening that is also always an act of interpretation or translation, an effort to render collaborators' understandings sensible to those who were not present and/or may have never considered collaborators' sensibilities. Making sense, then, is a form of deep listening (Oliveros, 2005).

As described in the introduction, despite claims to the contrary, most forms of qualitative research still focus on seeing. This *ocularcentrism* is part of what gives a pivot to listening its strength. This is because most forms of qualitative sight are directionally from the researcher-outward rather than attending to the inverse, the endlessly nested and layered ecologies of research contexts to a researcher. For us, it is difficult to speak about decentering the human or being with any other thing in relation while retaining ocular metaphors that insist—both in terms of historical baggage and contemporary practice—that a researcher is the hub around which a research ecology spins.

Literal listening is what we do as qualitative researchers. We hear the sounds of education as they unfold, carrying intentional and unintentional curricula to students. We conduct interviews that involve listening to others; spend time in classrooms and other educational ecologies, hearing what happens; and we are constantly impacting our research processes and the educational ecologies in which they are situated in material, sonic fashion. We make noises of approval or concern, ask questions, and hear what is going on.

This is not to say that one should not or does not observe or attend to questions about how things look. Instead, it emphasizes that listening, whether it involves hearing others or recognizing and describing relationships, is a fundamental aspect of what we do. If qualitative research rests on the belief that numbers are ideas, that our understandings of education are inherently subjective, and that we are drawn to the ebb, flow, and nuance of lived experience, then the way things appear should be met with at least a healthy degree of critical reflexivity—if not circumspection. Walter has documented our historical antecedents in education in multiple places (e.g., Gershon, 2011, 2017), and we have each respectively detailed the methodological shoulders on which our work stands (e.g., Gershon & Appelbaum, 2020; Gershon, 2024; Wozolek, 2023a, 2023b); what we offer here is a kind of recap of those histories, addressing how we use sound in our work in the following section.

Sonic Histories: Deep Listening to the Past to Think with/in the Present

In education, our work is part of a history of sonic scholarship from scholars such as Fredrick Erickson (e.g., 1982, 2003, 2004), Liora Bresler (e.g., 1998, 2005), Ted T. Aoki (e.g., 1991), and Greg Dimitradis (2009). It was Erickson, for example, who transcribed student talk as musical notation to note the skill and depth of students' linguistic improvisations in everyday classroom talk and interactions. Aoki underscores concern about the ocularcentric construction of educational understandings and processes, bringing jazz musicians to class to help future teachers better understand movement between structural and improvised elements of classroom lessons. Bresler documents how the Arts, in general, and music, specifically, can teach us important lessons about how to do (educational) qualitative research and the significance of sound in educational interactions. Dimitradis' (2009) book at the intersection of hip hop, pedagogy, and lived experience was crucial in the development of hip-hop education and how popular music can be a pathway for critical studies of education.

Outside of education, we are both indebted to scholars, musicians, and sound artists, such as Pauline Oliveros (2005), Audra McCartney (2016), Jennifer Stoever (2016), and Jonathan Sterne (2012). Oliveros, a queer Latinx musician, improviser, composer, and educator, was integral in composing and playing new and improvised musics from the early 1960s until her death in 2016. Oliveros' construct of deep listening, a mode of musical composition and sonic practice, was present in her theories and practice from her Sound Meditations (1974) through her positions on feminism and music with Fred Maus (1994) to her distillation of a lifetime of listening practice (2005). For Oliveros, listening with one's whole self is a life practice that also informs sonic ecologies that are conceptualized as musical interactions.

Jonathan Sterne continues in his work as one of the founders and more critical thinkers in the continuing consideration of the sounds, medias, theories, and culture. For example, Sterne has considered the history of sound production (2003), edited the *Sound Studies Reader*, (2012), and recently has written a multimodal, methodological, theoretical book about what he calls a political phenomenology of impairment that centers his own health experiences with voice and sound (Sterne, 2021). Jennifer Stoever is not only the author of one of the more immanently practical books for educators that uses DuBois to argue for what she calls a "sonic color line," but is also the founder and maintains the ever-useful *Sounding Out!* Blog, a place to find smart stuff about things sonic without genre, nation, field, or disciplinary boundaries (soundstudiesblog.com/).

We have both used Audra McCartney's (2016) moving and deeply thoughtful piece about soundwalking that utilizes a central question from Luce Irigaray to methodologically wonder: "How am I to listen to you?" This question, and its associated work, is perhaps the most influential and clear entree into how we methodologically consider and conceptualize sonic qualitative research. It is a question that is as much an ethical reminder as it encapsulates what it can mean to be/think/do sound in qualitative research.

This query places, front-and-center, questions of what Walter calls *directionality*: how, from where, and from whom or what knowledge flows. "How am I to listen to you?" is an insistence that research is an act of learning from outside to the researcher. McCartney's use of Irigaray's question is an expression of ethical commitments that the person who is in the role of "researcher" is clear that the beginning of a research relationship is predicated on consent and dignity (for more on this point, check Wozolek, 2023). This question also articulates a researcher's vulnerability and humility, that we, as qualitative researchers, are aware that we are here to learn from others and are asking for how we might approach our trajectories of engagement so that they are at once comfortable and sensible to our collaborators. Along similar lines, this question enunciates a kind of sonic omnidirectionality, underscoring the many possible directions listening might occur.

In a practical sense, the collaborative qualitative research we both conduct uses sound methodologies in ways that may appear to be about recording, but it is nearly always about listening: listening to our collaborators' narratives, to the sounds that form the ecologies affecting our collaborators' experiences, to our own sounds as they appear in our recordings, and again to the sounds of our collaborators as they share their feelings and ideas about the sounds we have gathered and shaped into forms for argumentative playback. In order to create our sonic scholarship, we use various forms of media to record, organize, and share the sounds we have gathered with collaborators.

These processes of listening take tens, if not hundreds, of hours over the course of a year-long project and its analysis. It is the equivalent of recording, engineering, editing, mastering, and distributing an album by us, often in addition to the 5000–10,000 word length expected in scholarly publications. We are not only constantly listening and re-listening to the audio we have gathered to get a sense of what we are hearing, but we are also shaping audio to tell particular narratives that, in keeping with our ethical commitments, are as sensible to potential listeners as they allow our collaborators to reside in dignity at their inclusion of our work.

Finally, it is our work in listening that again reminds us that what we have done is with others, and if we have done our jobs well, those sounds will resonate with others in ways that text and video, while valuable, cannot. For the same reasons that one cannot "scrub" forward on a radio narrative, listening to scholarship requires a particular kind of attention and focus. It is perhaps this that we value most of all—the ability to do work that reverberates in our listeners, affecting them in ways that neither they nor we can predict but are often greater than our anticipated expectations.

Suggestions for Further Reading

Gershon, W. S. (2017). *Sound curriculum: Sonic studies in educational theory, method, & practice.* Routledge.

McCartney, A. (2016). "How am I to listen to you?": Soundwalking, intimacy, and improvised listening. In G. Sidall & E. Waterman (Eds.), *Negotiated moments: Improvisation, sound, and subjectivity* (pp. 37–45). Duke University Press.

Sterne, J. (2012). *The sound studies reader*. Routledge.

Stoever, J. L. (2016). *The sonic color line: Race and the cultural politics of listening.* New York University Press.

Wozolek, B. (2023). *Educational necropolitics: A sonic ethnography of everyday racisms in U.S. schools.* Routledge.

References

Aoki, T. T. (1991). Five curriculum memos and a note for the next half-century. *Phenomenology and Pedagogy, 9*(1), 1–14.

Bearne, E., & Wolstencroft, H. (2007). *Visual approaches to teaching writing: Multimodal Literacy. 5–11.* Sage.

Bhattacharya, K. (2009). Othering research, researching the other: De/colonizing approaches to qualitative inquiry. In L.W. Perna (Ed.), *Higher education: Handbook of theory and research* (pp. 105–150). Springer.

Brearley, L. (2015). Deep listening and leadership: An Indigenous model of leadership and community development in Australia. In C. Voyager, L. Brearley, & B. Callou. (Eds.), *Restorying Indigenous leadership: Wise practices in community development* (pp. 91–127).

Bresler, L. (1998). The genre of school music and its shaping by meso, micro, and macro contexts. *Research Studies in Music Education, 11*(1), 2–18.

Bresler, L. (2005). What musicianship can teach educational research. *Music education research, 7*(2), 169–183.

Cahnmann-Taylor, M., & Siegesmund, R. (Eds.). (2017). *Arts-based research in education.* Routledge.

Carpenter, J. (2008). Metaphors in qualitative research: Shedding light or casting shadows? *Research in nursing & health, 31*(3), 274–282.

Dimitriadis, G. (2009). *Performing identity/performing culture: Hip hop as text, pedagogy, and lived practice.* Peter Lang.

Eisner, E. W. (1991). Rethinking literacy. *Educational Horizons, 69*(3), 120–128.

Erickson, F. (1982). Audiovisual records as a primary data source. *Sociological Methods & Research, 11*(2), 213–232.

Erickson, F. (2003). Some notes on the musicality of speech. In D. Tannen & J. A. Altis (Eds.), *Georgetown University Round Table on Languages and Linguistics (GURT) 2001* (pp. 274–282). Georgetown University Press.

Erickson, F. (2004). Demystifying data construction and analysis. *Anthropology & Education Quarterly, 35*(4), 486–493.

Gershon, W. S. (2011). Embodied knowledge: Sounds as educational systems. *Journal of Curriculum Theorizing, 27*(2), 66–81.

Gershon, W. S. (2017). *Sound curriculum: Sonic studies in educational theory, method, & practice.* Routledge.

Gershon, W. S. (2024). Sonically speaking: Soundwriting Inasthrough Qualitative Research. *International Review of Qualitative Research, 17*(3), 397–416. https://doi.org/10.1177/19408447241245689

Gershon, W. S. (forthcoming). *Sound methods: Qualitative research in, as, and through the sonic.* Routledge.

Gershon, W. S., & Appelbaum, P. M. (2020). *Sonic Studies in educational foundations: Echoes, reverberations, silences, noise.* Routledge, Taylor et Francis Group.

Knight, L. E. (2021). 'Creator gave us two ears and one mouth': Soundscapes as signifiers of environmental crisis at the intersections of Indigeneity and Acoustic Ecology. *Stream: Interdisciplinary Journal of Communication, 13*(1), 37–50.

Kohn, E. (2013). *How forests think: Toward an anthropology beyond the human.* University of California Press.

Leavy, P. (2020). *Method meets art: Arts-based research practice.* Guilford publications.

Lei, J. L. (2003). (Un) necessary toughness?: Those "Loud Black Girls" and those "Quiet Asian Boys". *Anthropology & Education Quarterly, 34*(2), 158–181.

McCartney, A. (2016). "How am I to listen to you?": Soundwalking, intimacy, and improvised listening. In G. Sidall & E. Waterman (Eds.), *Negotiated moments: Improvisation, sound, and subjectivity* (pp. 37–45). Duke University Press.

McKittrick, K. (2020). *Dear science and other stories.* Duke University Press.

Morris, M. (2016). *Pushout: The criminalization of Black girls in schools.* The New Press.

Noblit, G. W. (1999). *Particularities: Collected essays on ethnography and education*. Peter Lang Publishing.

Oliveros, P. (1974). *Sonic meditations*. Smith Publications.

Oliveros, P. (2005). *Deep listening: A composer's sound practice*. IUniverse.

Oliveros, P., & Maus, F. (1994). A conversation about feminism and music. *Perspectives of New Music, 32*(2), 174–193.

Plourde, L. (2019). *Tokyo listening: Sound and sense in a contemporary city*. Wesleyan University Press.

Robinson, D. (2020). *Hungry listening: Resonant theory for Indigenous sound studies*. University of Minnesota Press.

Smith, L. T. (1999/2021). *Decolonizing methodologies: Research and Indigenous peoples*. Bloomsbury Publishing.

Sterne, J. (2003). *The audible past: Cultural origins of sound reproduction*. Duke University Press.

Sterne, J. (2012). *The sound studies reader*. Routledge.

Sterne, J. (2021). *Diminished faculties: A political phenomenology of impairment*. Duke University Press.

Stoever, J. L. (2016). *The sonic color line: Race and the cultural politics of listening*. New York University Press.

Urrieta, L. (2009). *Working from within: Chicana and Chicano activist educators in whitestream schools*. University of Arizona Press.

Weheliye, A. G. (2023). *Feenin: R&B music and the materiality of BlackFem voices and technology*. Duke University Press.

Wolcott, H. (1990). On seeking-and rejecting-validity in qualitative research. In E. Eisner & A. Peshkin (Eds.), *Qualitative inquiry in education: The continuing debate* (pp. 121–152). Teachers College Press.

Wozolek, B. (2018). In 8100 again: The sounds of students breaking. *Educational Studies: A Journal of the American Educational Studies Association, 54*(4), 367–381. http://doi.org/10.1080/00131946.2018.1473869.

Wozolek, B. (2019). Mothering redux: Agency and joy in negotiating capitals of shame. *Journal of Gender Studies, 28*(8), 873–882.

Wozolek, B. (2023a). Echo Chambers of Oppression: Sound (ed) Understanding and Deep Listening through Sonic Ethnography. In Flashpoint Epistemology Volume 2 (pp. 62–83). Routledge.

Wozolek, B. (2023b). *Educational necropolitics: A sonic ethnography of everyday racisms in U.S. schools*. Routledge.

Wozolek, B. & Gershon, W.S. (2024). Sound traumas: Curricular attunements for care and educational understandings, *The Journal of Curriculum Theorizing, 39*(1a), 39(1b).

Chapter 5 Discussion Questions

1. Gershon and Wozolek argue that qualitative research in education remains overly reliant on ocular metaphors and practices. How might this *relational and literal myopia* hinder the ability to fully understand educational ecologies? Discuss specific examples from your own experiences or studies where an ocular-centric approach might have obscured deeper insights.
2. The authors suggest that sonic methodologies can challenge colonial practices in qualitative research. What are the potential risks and benefits of centering sonic practices in decolonial educational research? How can researchers ensure that such methods honor the dignity and agency of collaborators?
3. In the chapter, Gershon and Wozolek frame listening as a fundamental ethical commitment in qualitative research. In what ways might a practice of "deep listening" reshape the dynamics of power, care, and justice in educational settings? How can educators and researchers cultivate habits of listening in their professional practice?
4. The authors highlight the labor-intensive nature of sonic scholarship, including recording, analyzing, and editing audio materials. Considering these challenges, how can institutions support researchers in adopting sonic methodologies? What might be the implications for how scholarship is evaluated and valued?

SIX

Disrupting the Self: Currere and the Journey Toward Inclusive Pedagogy

Shani Steyn

IN THE EVER-CHANGING LANDSCAPE OF education research, methodologies that champion personal reflection and narratives are increasingly being recognised for their capacity to bring about transformation. One such method is *currere*, offering a life-changing process for educators to engage in as they reflect on and reframe their pedagogical practices (Cary, 2006). This chapter describes the author's personal journey of using currere to transition from her exclusive teaching landscape during the apartheid political era to a more inclusive, culturally competent pedagogical approach in post-apartheid South Africa (Steyn, 2024). Serving a dual purpose, this chapter is both a narrative and a guide for students in education research, demonstrating the reality of using currere as a disruptive research method and a tool for professional development.

Understanding Currere

Currere represents a fundamental change in how we perceive educational experiences. It provides a method to explore the inner self in relation to the broader society, thereby enriching learning and understanding (Poetter, 2024). The term currere was formulated by William Pinar in the 1970s and is derived from the Latin root of the word curriculum. As Pinar (2019) explained, "*Currere*, the Latin infinitive of curriculum, means to run the course—the root of the word curriculum. It refers to the running (or lived experience) of the course, the temporal and subjective experience of educational engagement" (p. 35). Whereas traditionally, curriculum theories focus on the content and structure of education, currere focuses on curriculum as it is experienced by the educator (Pinar, 2019).

Currere challenges and changes the epistemological grounds on which educational research is normally entered (Poetter, 2024). It is not content with how things usually are but seeks new ground and meaning from the personal and historical as it relates to self and culture. With the epistemology of currere, Pinar (2009) explained that education researchers can do qualitative studies that redress the quantification in education and the wider culture.

This chapter introduces currere as a method for qualitative education research. The epistemology contends that the self is the fullest source of knowledge available to the human being in the context of their experience (Grumet, 1975). Currere brings the self to the forefront, using personal narratives as the primary data source for an epistemological exploration of one's identity and its influence on engaging with and acting upon the world. Researchers can perform the disruptive, dislocating, and empowering acts that critique the culture's assumptions and actions about authority, gender, race, and social inequalities (Grumet, 1975).

The potential of currere to address the changing nature of education in a world of continuous transformation requires a significant crossing of borders. According to Smith (2013), currere is a new style of criticality that departs from a mere expression of ideas and takes place with an active life, following educational issues, with the intention of providing real learning in teaching. Such an education can change the status quo, and society can be humanized.

Currere is a form of self-inquiry and is part of the intellectual tradition of philosophy in education. It offers a conceptual mode of criticism that positions individuals in educational settings as agents who self-author reality (D'Adamo, 2024). This movement is an ordinary dimension of human life that provides new approaches to understanding the lives of people in educational environments (Doerr & Doerr, 2004). In other words, currere is an imaginative contemplation of the collective life of a living being.

How is Currere Used in Research?

Currere comprises a reflective process where the educator moves through cyclical phases of regression, progression, analysis, and synthesis (Pinar, 2015). As Pinar explained, these phases enable individuals to delve into past experiences, imagine future possibilities, analyze their current context, and synthesize these insights to transform their practice.

Regressive

In this phase, educators are encouraged to remember and reflect on past experiences, specifically those that have impacted their current beliefs and practices (Pinar, 2015). This process requires an intentional slowing down and taking a step back as the educator delves into historical contexts that have shaped their assumptions and biases, allowing the memories and accompanying emotions to surface (Stewart & Stewart, 2020). By probing personal and professional memories, the educator can uncover formative experiences that have influenced their present-day pedagogies while simultaneously recognizing the emotional and psychological impact of past experiences. This phase is not merely a trip down memory lane but an intentional remembering and analysis of these formative realities to gain better insight and understanding of their current teacher identity (Grumet, 1975).

Progressive

The educator focuses on envisioning the future during this phase as they are prompted to reimagine their pedagogies, looking ahead at the potential and possibilities that are in store for them in their teaching career (Pinar, 2015). Educators are required to think creatively and without restriction about what could be (Kanu, 2006). This stage involves dreaming big about new classroom teaching practices and emerging pedagogical methods that could transform their professional lives, imagining different goals and student outcomes and what their ultimate contribution to educational advancements and future generations could be. To assist with this moment, it helps to answer the question: "What would I like to be remembered for, within the field of education, when I am no longer on earth?"

Analytical

At this stage, the educator critically analyzes their current situation, examining the influence of past experiences and future aspirations on their present practices and beliefs (Pinar, 2015). A crucial aspect of this phase is that educators begin to understand the reciprocity between their past experiences, their present pedagogy, and their future ambitions (Kuhnke, 2023). This moment calls for a comprehensive contextual analysis of institutional policies, student demographics, and available resources that shape the current educational landscape. Equally important is the practice of self-evaluation, in which educators critically assess the effectiveness of their teaching in relation to their educational goals (Morris, 2015). Engaging in this dual reflection—on both context and self—supports a deeper critique of the status quo and helps identify areas in need of improvement and growth.

Synthetical

This final phase encompasses the integration of perceptions and insights from the previous three phases to develop a coherent understanding of one's practice and to facilitate the development of a plan for action to transform one's pedagogical self, both professionally and personally (Pinar, 2015). This involves accomplishing an in-depth and interrelated perception of how various aspects of their personal and professional lives impact their teaching. This stage ends with formulating actionable strategies to transform and change pedagogical practices and committing to ongoing self-development. A crucial moment during this stage is the embracing of the inevitability of change that is required to grow both personally and professionally (Steyn, 2020).

By gradually and steadily transitioning through these stages, educators begin to develop a more meaningful awareness of themselves and their teaching, which in turn gives rise to more effective teaching.

My Currere Journey

Reflecting on Apartheid Education

My formative years in education were marked by systemic racial segregation and discrimination, as I was born and raised during the apartheid regime in South Africa (Steyn, 2020). It is no secret that the education system was designed and implemented to reinforce racial hierarchies, with huge discrepancies in resources and opportunities available to students based on their race (Steyn, 2024). As an educator, I initially perpetuated these practices, largely because they were all I knew.

Reflecting on this period during the regressive phase raised emotional pain that needed to be acknowledged and processed. I found myself vividly remembering segregated classrooms, biased curricula, and discriminatory practices, recalling the discomfort and cognitive dissonance that went with these memories (Steyn, 2020, 2024). Recognizing the deep-rooted injustices of the system, I realized how important this phase was, not only in understanding but also in acknowledging the depth at which these experiences had impacted my beliefs and teaching methods.

Imagining an Inclusive Future

Moving into the progressive phase brought immediate relief as I began to envision a different kind of education—letting my imagination run its own course. Filled with the prospect of inclusive, equitable, and culturally responsive education, I imagined classrooms where all students, irrespective of their background, felt valued, heard, and supported (Steyn, 2020). In my reimagining, the curricula embraced and celebrated diversity as well as fostered critical thinking in respect of social justice issues.

My vision was inspired by both the ideals and promises of the new democratic regime that emerged in post-apartheid South Africa and the global movement towards inclusive education. I saw schools as potential catalysts for change, where students could acquire both academic content and skills as well as dispositions to build a more equitable society (Steyn, 2020, 2024).

Analyzing the Present Reality

During the analytical phase, I evaluated my present pedagogical landscape, analyzing the ways in which my prior schooling under the apartheid regime influenced my present attitudes and actions. I acknowledged that even with my best efforts to be more inclusive, I continued to act in ways that excluded certain students (Steyn, 2020). My perspectives still contained racial blind spots that resulted in prejudicial thought-processing and behaviour.

At the same time, I investigated South Africa's larger educational landscape, noticing that despite the nation's great progress towards educational justice, numerous obstacles remained. Persistent racial conflicts and unequal access to resources are apartheid legacies that still persist. Comprehending these facts was necessary to firmly establish my vision within the real world of my profession.

Synthesizing Insights for Transformation

To be equipped to create a strategy for transforming my pedagogy, this phase involved the combining of my analysis of the present, my vision for the future, and my reflections on the past. This meant changing my strategy in a few significant ways:

First, I made a commitment to keep studying other cultures, immersing myself in cross-cultural friendships and fostering safe spaces for brave and critical dialogue in my classroom. Although I could not change the core curriculum content, I made a point to be creative and include previously underrepresented historical narratives and voices.

Second, I began implementing a variety of teaching methods that included individualized instruction and collaborative learning to benefit every student, fostering an atmosphere where each student felt valued and comfortable.

Third, by using currere and other reflective tools, I integrated reflection into my practice on a regular basis to evaluate and refine my teaching. This required asking colleagues and students for input and being willing to accept criticism and change accordingly.

Last, and probably most importantly, due to the autobiographical nature of currere, I was encouraged to consider the lived experiences of my students, fostering empathy and a greater appreciation for their histories and different cultural perspectives.

The Impact of Currere on Transformation

Professional Growth

Utilizing currere as a research method greatly improved my career development. I was able to move beyond surface-level tweaks in my teaching strategies to create significant and long-lasting changes to the way I teach. I became conscious of my ingrained biases and was able to confront and redefine them. By critically analyzing my past and present, I was able to identify behaviors and practices that supported injustices. Through this process, I became a more reflective and purposeful teacher. Due to the cyclical nature of currere, provision is made for a framework that includes ongoing professional improvement and adaptation. In the dynamic field of education, where there is a constant rise of new challenges and opportunities, currere is a valuable method for research.

Personal Growth

On a personal level, currere facilitated a process of deracialization and cultural competence. As I reflected on my experiences of apartheid education, I was forced to confront my own racist attitudes and beliefs. It was a humbling and, at times, uncomfortable process, but it was also profoundly liberating. By acknowledging and addressing these false assumptions and beliefs, I was able to develop a more inclusive and empathetic worldview.

This personal growth was essential for my professional transformation. It is no secret that a teacher's beliefs and attitudes inevitably influence their teaching. Becoming more culturally competent and inclusive in my personal life made me a better teacher and a better advocate for my students.

Implementing Currere in Education Research

For students in education research, currere offers a unique and valuable methodology. Implementing currere involves several steps:

First, identify a specific aspect of your teaching or educational experience to explore. This could be a particular challenge, a significant event, or a general area of interest.

Second, use the four stages of currere to guide your reflection. Take your time with each stage, allowing yourself to fully explore your experiences and insights.

A great idea is to keep a journal or create a narrative to document your reflections. This documentation will be valuable for both your own learning and for sharing your findings with others.

During the analysis and synthesis phases, critically analyze your reflections to identify patterns, themes, and insights. Integrate these findings to develop a clear and comprehensive understanding of your focus area and to inform your practice going forward.

Currere as a Disruptive Research Method

Currere, as an autobiographical research method, is a powerful tool for disrupting systems of oppression and empowering participants. It disrupts traditional notions of research by placing the individual's experience at the center and by recognizing the value of narrative and emotions in the research process. By engaging in the cyclical nature of currere, educators can identify and unpack subconscious biases and cultural blind spots, recognize organizational structures that perpetuate injustices, and challenge them to bring about transformation (Pinar, 2019).

Currere allows educators to develop a holistic understanding of their practice by considering the past, present, and the future. This comprehensive perspective is essential for meaningful transformation. Through continual reflection, educators begin to understand how past injustices still influence the present. They are encouraged to become agents of change, to move from merely understanding to challenging and taking action to disempower these narratives, thereby promoting a more equitable education landscape (Pinar, 2015). By continually engaging in this reflexive process, educators become more aware of their students' diverse experiences and perspectives, which fosters a deeper understanding and empathy for the impact of systemic inequities.

The process of currere allowed me to offer an honest and vulnerable recognition of privilege and exclusivity that resulted in the disruption of deep-seated racial bias and assumptions, the unveiling of racial blind spots, and confronting the discourse that South African white educators are, overtly or covertly, perpetuating systemic racism within schools (Steyn, 2020). The theoretical concepts of currere were used to analyze my lived educational experiences within the apartheid regime and to initiate my journey towards deracialization and transformation of my current pedagogical practice.

Self-Reflexivity: How is Currere Different?

While many qualitative methodologies incorporate self-reflexivity as a central component, the distinctiveness of currere lies in its deep engagement with the personal, temporal, and narrative dimensions of one's lived educational experiences, setting it apart from methodologies such as action research and autoethnography.

The currere method is highly introspective and rooted in the time-related unfolding of personal experiences, with a focus on subjective curriculum and its implications. This element of self-reflexivity is centered on how one's identity is formed through educational encounters across time. It explores the individual's internal curriculum and is deeply concerned with how those experiences affect pedagogical practice. Time and personal history are crucial in shaping this reflective process. It is not just about reflecting on one's actions (like in action research) or cultural identity (like in autoethnography) but understanding how one's entire life experience is a curriculum itself.

In action research, self-reflexivity is primarily collaborative and problem-solving-oriented. Action researchers reflect on their practices to change and improve those practices within a specific context, often with others, whereas currere is more about exploring and understanding personal experiences in a non-linear, narrative fashion. Reflexivity in currere is not about change that occurs instantly but about deeper self-understanding and transformation that informs one's teaching and being.

In autoethnography, another qualitative method that demands deep self-reflexivity, the focus is more explicitly on situating the self within a broader cultural context. Autoethnographers reflect on personal experiences to explore cultural, political, and social dimensions of identity. Thus, while both autoethnography and currere engage deeply with personal narratives, autoethnography tends to frame these narratives in terms of cultural critique and sociopolitical commentary. In contrast, currere emphasizes how personal experiences inform and transform one's pedagogical journey, often through a more individualized introspective lens.

In highlighting the unique self-reflexive process of currere, it becomes clear that while action research and autoethnography offer valuable reflective practices, currere provides a deeply personal and temporally nuanced exploration of one's educational journey, enabling a profound transformation of both self and pedagogy.

Conclusion

The concept of currere, developed by William Pinar (2015), offers a transformative approach to education that disrupts traditional power structures and empowers participants to critically examine their own experiences and identities. The author's journey from apartheid education to inclusive education in South Africa illustrates the profound impact that currere can have on both professional and personal growth. By embracing this method, educators can develop a deeper understanding of their practice, enhance their overall competence, and become more effective advocates for their students (Steyn, 2024). For students in education research, currere offers a valuable tool for exploring and addressing the complex challenges of teaching and learning in diverse and dynamic contexts (Le Grange, 2019). By centering students' lived experiences, currere encourages a shift from the *banking model* of education to a more dynamic, collaborative, and emancipatory process (Freire, 2018). This pedagogical approach aligns with the principles of critical consciousness, which seeks to challenge the dominant narrative and equip learners with the tools to recognize and dismantle oppressive systems (Wang, 2010).

Suggestions for Further Reading and References

Adams, S. R., & Buffington-Adams, J. (2020). On/beyond currere. *The Currere Exchange Journal, 4*(2), 63–70.

Cary, L. J. (2006). From currere to curriculum spaces: Bringing together curriculum theory and educational research. *Journal of Curriculum and Pedagogy, 3*(2), 148–167.

Corey, S. M. (1954). Action research in education. *The Journal of Educational Research, 47*(5), 375–380.

D'Adamo, K. N. (2024). *Currere as contemporary art: Creative research methods for teacher self-reflection.* [Unpublished doctoral dissertation]. University of Nebraska, Lincoln.

Doerr, M., & Doerr, M. N. (2004). *Currere and the environmental autobiography: A phenomenological approach to the teaching of ecology* (Vol. 4). Peter Lang.

Freire, P. (2018). *Pedagogy of the oppressed: 50th anniversary edition* (M. B. Ramos, Trans.). Bloomsbury Academic.

Grumet, M. R. (1975). Existential and phenomenological foundations of currere: Self-report in curriculum inquiry. Paper Presented at the American Educational Research Assn. (AERA). Washington, DC.

Jack-Malik, S., & Kuhnke, J. L. (2020). Shame on course evaluations: Currere and duoethnography. *The Currere Exchange Journal, 4*(2), 71–82.

Kanu, Y. (2006). 'Currere' to the rescue? Teachers as 'amateur intellectuals' in a knowledge society. *Journal of the Canadian Association for Curriculum Studies, 4*(2), 101–122.

Kuhnke, J. L. (2023). Gratitude journaling practice: A reflective currere. *The Currere Exchange Journal, 7*(1), 42–54.

Le Grange, L. (2019). Currere's active force and the concept of Ubuntu. In C. Hébert, N. Ng-A-Fook, A. Ibrahim, & B. Smith (Eds.), *Internationalizing curriculum studies: Histories, environments, and critiques* (pp. 207–228). Springer.

McQueen, J. (2017). Tell me I matter: Currere as a curricular journey. *Currere Exchange Journal, 1*(2), 79–84.

Morris, M. A. R. L. A. (2015). Currere as subject matter. In M. F. He, B. D. Shultz, & W. H. Shubert (2015). *The SAGE Guide to Curriculum in Education* (pp. 104–109).

Pinar, W. F. (2009). The primacy of the particular. In L. J. Waks & E. C. Short (Eds). *Leaders in curriculum studies: Intellectual self-portraits* (Vol. 2) Brill. (pp. 143–152).

Pinar, W. F. (2015). *Educational experience as lived: Knowledge, history, alterity: The selected works of William F. Pinar*. Routledge.

Pinar, W. F. (2019). *What is curriculum theory?* Routledge.

Pinar, W. F. (2022). *A praxis of presence in curriculum theory: Advancing currere against cultural crises in education*. Routledge.

Poetter, T. S. (2024). *Curriculum fragments: A currere journey through life processes*. Taylor & Francis.

Pole, C., & Morrison, M. (2003). *Ethnography for education*. McGraw-Hill Education (UK)

Schubert, W. H. (2009). Currere and disciplinarity in curriculum studies: Possibilities for education research. *Educational Researcher, 38*(2), 136–140. https://doi.org/10.3102/0013189x09332136

Smith, B. A. (2013). Currere and critical pedagogy: Thinking critically about self-reflective methods. *TCI (Transnational Curriculum Inquiry), 10*(2), 3–16.

Smythe, W. E., & Murray, M. J. (2000). Owning the story: Ethical considerations in narrative research. *Ethics & Behavior, 10*(4), 311–336.

Stewart, A., & Stewart, A. (2020). Developing place-responsive pedagogy in outdoor environmental education: A rhizomatic curriculum autobiography. In A. Stewart & A. Stewart (Eds.), *Living curriculum: Currere* (pp. 29–36). Springer.

Steyn, S. (2020). *Currere as deracialisation: An autobiographical reflection of a white teacher in multicultural post-apartheid South African classrooms* [Unpublished doctoral dissertation]. Stellenbosch: Stellenbosch University.

Steyn, S. (2024). *Currere from Apartheid to inclusion: Building culturally responsive pedagogies in post-apartheid South Africa*. Taylor & Francis.

Van den Berg & Gerth, S. (2024). From currere to ambire: An ambient curriculum. *JCT: Journal of Curriculum Theorizing, 39*.

Wang, H. (2010). The temporality of currere, change, and teacher education. *Pedagogies: An International Journal, 5*(4), 275–285.

Chapter 6 Discussion Questions

1. How does currere challenge traditional educational research paradigms, and in what ways does it act as a disruptive methodology to address systemic inequities in education? Reflect on how this approach could be applied within your own teaching or research context to confront implicit biases or cultural blind spots.
2. The regressive, progressive, analytical, and synthetical phases of currere facilitate deep self-reflection and transformation for educators. How do these phases enable a comprehensive understanding of one's educational journey, and which phase might be the most challenging or impactful for you?
3. Considering Steyn's use of currere to navigate apartheid-era exclusionary practices, how might this methodology support educators in addressing culturally or historically complex contexts? Discuss its potential to foster inclusive and equitable pedagogies in diverse educational settings.
4. How does currere differ from methodologies such as action research and autoethnography in its approach to self-reflexivity and transformation? In what scenarios might currere be a more suitable methodology, and what unique contributions does it offer to educational research and practice?

SEVEN

A Collective Disruption: Doing Duoethnography with/as Black Women

Asha S. Winfield, Nabila Mushtarin, Hope Hickerson, Anglesia Brown, and DeShara C. Doub

Making space for Black women to be in scholarly and culturally responsive qualitative research conversations for academic research may look like a melody of experiences soundtracked by song:

> *Go Meg' (Baow); Go Meg' (Ah); Get 'em Glo' (Ayy); Get 'em Glo' (Huh); Get 'em Glo (Woo)'*
>
> —Wanna Be by GloRilla, Megan thee Stallion, and Cardi B. (Woods, et al, 2024).

> *Count on me through thick and thin; A friendship that will never end; When you are weak I will be strong; Helping you to carry on; Call on me, I will be there; Don't be afraid; Please believe me when I say; Count on me*
>
> (Whitney Houston & CeCe Winans, 1996).

Research methods, when utilized in ways that center the participants' lived experiences, allow for readers, participants, and researchers to explore a list of major life events, including the impacts of histories of oppression and silencing and the creativity that it birthed in a number of ways. Our research team has employed the utilization of duoethnography to empower our participants as co-authors and co-conspirators in our research efforts toward more visible and equitable work. In this chapter, we discuss how it has been defined and used in research across several disciplines, and then we discuss how we work with the method to tell more complex and holistic narratives in interdisciplinary community research with Black women.

What is Duoethnography?

Scholars have defined and utilized duoethnography in diverse ways to challenge established norms of academic inquiry. For example, Sawyer and Norris (2013) describe duoethnography as a collaborative research method involving two or more researchers with contrasting backgrounds investigating a phenomenon to challenge and reframe existing systems or beliefs. In the specific context of this paper, duoethnography takes on a distinct purpose. Here, it is defined as a collaboration of Black and Brown women scholars who identify themselves as Sister Scholars sharing overlapping experiences to create more inclusive ways of knowing to transform the way scholarly expertise and information are brought to academia (Garrett et al., 2024; Teasdell et al., 2021). This approach seeks not only to generate new insights but also to challenge and transform the traditional ways in which scholarly expertise and information are disseminated and valued within academic settings (Garrett et al., 2024; Teasdell et al., 2021). The practice of duoethnography encourages our Sister Scholars to acknowledge and celebrate their subjectivities and positionalities during the knowledge production process.

Duoethnography is more than a methodological approach. It is a critical epistemological stance as it challenges the status quo through highlighting marginalized voices and perspectives (Brown, 2024; Teasdell et al., 2021). Therefore, duoethnography serves as a catalyst for the authors of this paper, our mother-authors, and other Sister Scholars/sista scholars to collectively disrupt traditional ways of knowing in academia (Garrett et al., 2024; Keikelame & Swartz, 2019).

For our group, duoethnography serves as a novel methodological approach that disrupts established norms in academic inquiry and knowledge production. Defined as a collaborative effort among Black and Brown women scholars, duoethnography enriches scholarly discourse by centering marginalized voices and perspectives, reshaping how intellectual work is disseminated and valued. This approach generates new insights and fosters inclusivity and reflexivity in knowledge production, encouraging SisterScholars to celebrate and explore their subjectivities and positionalities. By disrupting conventional paradigms of academic knowledge, duoethnography contributes to the scholarly community and advocates for broader social change, affirming the significance and impact of diverse perspectives in shaping academic discourse and beyond.

How Is Duoethnography Used In Our Research?

> "We chose this format to not only engage our own ways of knowing as it relates to Black women's health and health storytelling but also bring light to our shared and individual experiences of love, blood, and struggle. It is birthed from the sometimes broken bodies, broken systems, and beautiful Black women that found a way(s) to survive in the midst of it all." (Winfield et al., 2024)

As described in the previously quoted passage, duoethnography has been used as a way to tell stories that otherwise might have remained silenced. In the aforementioned scholarship, we had the privilege of truth-telling with our mothers. The technique can't be described as interviewing because the experience was a sharing of deep emotions that couldn't be captured simply in a question-and-answer format. There first had to be love, then trust, and finally, a cathartic release of truth.

Traditionally, older Black mothers may find it difficult to talk about past hurts and injustices because cultural norms, *back in their day*, dictated that certain topics remained quiet for fear of reproach and discrimination (Winfield et al., 2024). As such, asking our mothers to participate in the duoethnographic process was a heavy ask, but one of our mothers answered simply because of their desire to see us successful in our work. Thus began the process of eliciting their stories—a process of seeking, acknowledging, and validating their experiences that ultimately healed long-buried wounds. In addition, as subject matter experts of their own lived experiences, our mothers were included as authors, which provoked feelings of pride and joy for their bravery to tell their stories. Duoethnography allowed us to give back to our mothers while also providing an example of how this method can not only be used as a research tool, but also as a vehicle for connection and relationship-building for other mothers and daughters.

Our mothers were not the only benefactors of this process. As researchers, we would be remiss not to mention how duoethnography was used to affirm the necessity and power of qualitative story-telling in academia. For populations that aren't in the majority, seeing their narratives depicted in black and white can provide them the confidence to open doors previously believed to be closed. Plainly speaking, numbers and statistics certainly have their place in research; however, qualitative methods are equally important because they allow the subject to be humanized in ways that resonate with readers. As storytellers on a quest to turn up the volume for those whose voices have historically been muted, one way we do that is through the mutually beneficial process of duoethnography.

Foundational Texts and Important Theorists

Duoethnography is a qualitative, dialogue-based research method where two or more researchers work to critique and investigate sociocultural issues (Sawyer & Norris, 2013). Sawyer and Norris coined the term in 2004 to define a form of dialogic and reflexive autoethnography to represent their own stories and use frames to examine meaning-making. Duoethnographers examine stories, personal experiences, memories, and artifacts to provide a critical perspective on issues related to their identities (Breault, 2016; Sawyer & Norris, 2009). According to Sawyer and Norris (2009), this theory is loosely based on Maurice Merleau-Ponty's (1962) belief that "consciousness and culture influence experience and that experiences are always mediated by individual and cultural meanings given to past experiences, duoethnography is an examination of the process through which individuals make meaning out of a particular phenomenon" (p. 127).

Being a dialogic process, duoethnography disrupts metanarratives that can emerge from our own writing and sees the self not as the source but as the site of research (Breault, 2016). The dialogue between two researchers opens up the possibility to re-interpret and create new knowledge because each researcher pushes the other to let go of their beliefs and interpret their experiences in a new light (Latz & Murray, 2012).

The method has evolved over the past ten years, expanding researchers' understanding of, and engagement with, this collaborative methodology (Burleigh & Burm, 2022). In the earlier conceptions, Norris and Sawyer described four tenets: (1) avoiding a prescriptive approach, (2) making individual voice explicit, (3) change of perspective, and (4) differences being the strength (Breault, 2016; Norris & Sawyer, 2004; Sawyer & Norris, 2013). Our process with duoethnography is perfectly captured here as a "practice from within it—but through the eyes of one distant to it—to provide a new and destabilizing lens. It is done with at least two practitioners working together in tandem in a dialogic format emphasizing differences in perception between these inquirers. In it, inquirers examine not just the present situation, but also their past personal history leading to the present, as well as the critical genealogies of beliefs and discourses within their family and early situations" that affected their subsequent actions (Sawyer & Norris, 2016, p. 2). We avoided a prescriptive approach and made individual voices explicit by engaging our mothers and making their experiences the central focus, so much so that they are listed as co-authors for that body of work.

We didn't follow any set rules when we approached our mothers with this idea. We had to navigate our mothers' initial apprehensions and periodic feelings of pain and shame as only we knew how . . . as loving, patient, and understanding daughters that were wholly there for them throughout the process. Trust is imperative in duoethnography. That absolute trust between the duos paved the way for our mothers to share their innermost thoughts without fear that their words would be distorted or taken out of context. In addition, we felt that a 'back-and-forth' format between one mother/daughter segment and the other duo offered that change of perspective necessary to show that Black mothers are not a monolith but often share similar experiences. Last, we embraced the tenet of differences being the strength by focusing our dialogue on topics that typically aren't discussed. It's *hard* for Black mothers of a certain age to discuss women's reproductive issues with their daughters. It's *difficult* for many Black mothers to admit to perceived shortcomings in their parenting and potentially open themselves up to criticism from unknown readers. We decided that embracing the hard, difficult, and different was more important than continuing to remain silent and unhealed.

In their work, Burleigh & Burm (2022) note that Norris & Sawyers' 2012 article expanded the tenets of this method and included the following [our own practical emphases applied]:

1. **Life as a curriculum**—*what we create, we reify. Someone's life and history are curriculum and always have been. Our own research, now published, is becoming the lessons for other scholars and learners across multiple disciplines.*
2. **Polyvocal and dialogic**—*multiple voices in conversation with their lived experiences is duoethnography with equity. Amplifying the voices of our mothers' experiences through conversation was key for our research on Black women's health across generations and the stories we tell.*

3. **Deliberate juxtaposition**—*Positioning the voices/experiences with and against each other but not in competition is essential; only highlight the variety and variability of lived experiences through comparison, not ranking.*
4. **Differences are articulated and discussed to interrogate and disrupt stories**—*Our stories grow and transform through our meaningful dialogue and disruptions with one another. We end up interrogating policies, people, and reform instead of each other and truths.*
5. **Question meanings held about the past to invite reconceptualization**—*Our questions of each other and the topic help us to explore the past, current, and future implications of our knowing. Create questions that help co-authors to make different considerations and connections.*
6. **Universal truths are not sought**—*We are not seeking to eliminate one truth(s) for the sake of one truth. Instead, we invite a harmony or blending of chorded notes for our research song.*
7. **A form of praxis**—*Dueothnography is a practice with intentional research goals making it different from interviews, focus groups, and some narrative inquiries.*
8. **An ethical stance is a negotiated space**—*Reproducing an ethics of care in the space we curate makes a safe place for research exploration.*
9. **Deep layers of trust grow over time and allow disclosure and rigorous conversation**—*Based on the ethical space that is created, and rapport that is grown from sharing, trust is built with each conversation, adding to depth of disclosure. It may not happen in one sitting as with the research with our mothers.* (Winfield et al, 2024)

In the earliest examples of duoethnographic research, authors used the method to reconstruct meanings of concepts such as sexual orientation (Sawyer & Norris, 2004) and beauty from a decolonial perspective (Shelton & McDermott, 2012). The method has since then served as a tool for dialogic inquiry in educational settings, e.g., cross-cultural teaching and learning experiences (e.g., Koonce & Lewis, 2020; Karas & Uchihara, 2021), and negotiating own identities, such as authenticity in own racial identities (Ashlee & Quaye, 2021) or examining own beliefs as an academic scholar (Sawyer & Norris, 2016). More recent scholarly works have utilized the method to fill a gap in qualitative research on health concerns, such as reproductive trauma

(Brigance & Brigance, 2023) or intergenerational health disparities within the Black community (Winfield et al., 2024).

Disrupting Systems of Oppression and Empowering Participants

Duoethnography represents a dynamic and interdisciplinary methodological approach that transcends traditional boundaries within research. It offers a transformative pathway by spotlighting these underrepresented voices, providing a platform for authentic storytelling, and challenging the status quo (Garrett et al., 2024; Keikelame & Swartz, 2019; Sawyer & Norris, 2013; Teasdell et al., 2021).

While the authorship and subsequent voices of racialized, minoritized participants have historically been under-recorded within research, the opportunity to spotlight these unique voices through methodologies such as duoethnography automatically creates space for those often feeling disempowered within the world. These narratives provide firsthand accounts of those directly impacted by systems that are often oppressive, a side not often published in academic journals. The barrier between the researcher and the layperson is lifted, providing an additional opportunity for system disruption that often exudes power and control. The utilization of duoethnography encourages diverse thought and uplifts the voice of the disenfranchised, which promotes self-determination and personal agency.

As duoethnography utilizes a social justice framework, there is a natural intersection within the field of social work. While the genesis of the social work profession stems from the multidisciplinary principles from fields like science and medicine (Giterman, 2014), the mission is always centered on the welfare of the underserved. With this tenant in mind, utilizing duoethnography within the social work profession ensures and even demands that disruption occurs. Within the strategic goals of the social work profession through The Council on Social Work Education (CSWE), social workers should engage diverse communities through promoting research that advances social justice (CSWE, 2020).

Duoethnography is a powerful methodological approach and epistemology within higher education that actively disrupts entrenched academic norms (Garrett et al., 2024; Keikelame & Swartz, 2019; Teasdell et al., 2021). It removes the notion that Black and Brown women scholars need permission to produce knowledge. Duoethnography methodologically and epistemologically confronts and dismantles systemic oppression within higher education. It not only generates new and innovative insights but also advocates for broader social change by amplifying marginalized voices and fostering a more inclusive scholarly environment where the stories and humanity of Black and Brown women scholars are respected and protected in their resistance against oppression.

Protecting the stories, humanity, and resistance of Black and Brown women authentically in duoethnography involves several fundamental principles and practices. Duoethnography prioritizes the genuine representation of participants' voices and experiences, ensuring participant narratives are heard without distortion or manipulation. Respect for agency and consent is paramount to sharing and using stories throughout the research process. Cultural sensitivity is crucial to honoring participants' diverse backgrounds and identities, requiring researchers to navigate potential power dynamics thoughtfully and remain mindful of their biases (Johnson, 2015; Teasdell et al., 2021). Addressing power imbalances involves transparent communication about the research process, allowing participants to actively shape research agendas and fostering equitable partnerships (Johnson, 2015; Teasdell et al., 2021).

Maintaining confidentiality through stringent privacy measures, and anonymizing identities when necessary, safeguards participants from potential repercussions. Ethical reflection and reflexivity guide researchers in continually examining their biases and ethical responsibilities, ensuring the research remains respectful and aligned with the scholars' interests. Duoethnography also aims to recognize scholars through representation, validating their perspectives, promoting their self-determination, and acknowledging their agency in contributing to knowledge production and advocacy efforts. Long-term engagement with participants beyond data collection fosters trust and mutual respect, enabling researchers to support ongoing struggles against oppression and amplify participants' voices within academic and broader societal contexts (Brown, 2024; Johnson, 2015).

By upholding these principles, duoethnography authentically protects Black and Brown women's stories, humanity, and resistance, ensuring their voices are respected, heard, and impactful. Participants in duoethnography reclaim agency in shaping research processes and outcomes, validating their perspectives and safeguarding narratives that have often been distorted or overlooked.

As a social justice framework, duoethnography critically examines social inequalities and actively works towards rectification, aligning with the ethical responsibilities of higher education to advocate for marginalized communities and dismantle unjust systems (Brown, 2024; Johnson, 2024). Duoethnography disrupts traditional academic practices by advocating for a reflexive research approach, compelling researchers to reflect critically on their biases and positionalities. This process promotes greater equity and transparency in knowledge creation, fundamentally challenging existing hierarchies of knowledge production within academia.

At its core, duoethnography enables these scholars to share their lived experiences authentically, challenging the historical tendency in traditional research to either silence or superficially acknowledge their voices (Teasdell et al., 2021). By centering the narratives of marginalized groups, duoethnography directly confronts systemic oppression within academic research, illuminating and challenging power dynamics that perpetuate marginalization (Brown, 2024; Johnson, 2015; Teasdell et al., 2021). Through collaborative efforts across diverse backgrounds and viewpoints, this approach constructs knowledge that is inherently inclusive, expanding the understanding of complex phenomena beyond conventional narratives.

Finally, duoethnography emerges as an interdisciplinary transformative and indispensable methodological approach within academic research, particularly in its ability to challenge and disrupt traditional norms (Sawyer & Norris, 2013). By spotlighting the narratives of marginalized groups, such as Black and Brown women scholars, duoethnography validates their lived experiences and confronts systemic oppression entrenched within academia (Garrett et al., 2024; Teasdell et al., 2021). This approach expands the understanding of complex social phenomena and advocates for broader social change by amplifying historically silenced or misrepresented voices. Through its commitment to ethical reflexivity and inclusive practices, duoethnography paves the way for a more equitable and transparent knowledge production process where diverse perspectives are recognized and celebrated (Sawyer & Norris, 2013; Teasdell et al., 2021). As Black and Brown women scholars continue to engage with duoethnography, its impact will foster a more inclusive scholarly environment, ensuring that marginalized communities' stories, humanity, and resistance are respected, heard, and valued.

Recommendations and Reflections

As interdisciplinary scholars in and across multiple fields, women of color, and emerging voices in the academic world, we found it most beneficial and meaningful to share the experiences of our participants, co-researchers, co-conspirators, and co-authors in non-traditional ways. To put it another way, *we put their name on the paper*. Too often, researchers parachute into communities of color for their horror stories, even receiving grant funding to do the work, and leave dust in the wind as they hang and decorate their university offices with awards for doing the *good work*. Conducting this type of research with our mothers allowed us to accomplish a few goals:

- ***Disrupt the sound of academia:*** Turning the mic on for our co-authors/co-participants is how we set the standard for other scholars doing intergenerational, multicultural, and identity-based research. The sound of academia has, in recent years, with more disruptive research, begun to sound musical in nature along the slick-back edges of the body of research. In recent studies, duoethnography in education has also included slam poetry (Wilson & Shields, 2019), has been used in Black hair studies with arts-based methods (Brown & Gilbert, 2021), and has been part of dance therapy studies with scholars of color (Thomas & Blanc, 2021) and a dialogue across women of color searching for culture in art education courses (Sions & Coleman, 2019).
- ***Disrupt the source:*** Disrupt the idea that knowledge production can only be derived from degreed individuals with a record of higher education. Too often, the idea that the source, or the *who* about *whom*, can produce knowledge is problematized and trivialized. This way of thinking continues to divide us rather than allow us to recognize the potential for learning and enlightenment from those who survived to tell the tales.
- ***Disrupt the access to this work:*** A goal of duoethnography is to disrupt the status quo; this cannot be done only behind the paywall of academic texts. We seek out more opportunities for open access journals where those who need this knowledge the most, like our neighbors, community members, and policy makers looking to change things for the better, can engage with and share it with others.

- ***Disrupt the history:*** This work provided us with the opportunity to see more clearly how intersectionality and identity impact lived experiences. As we listened to our mothers' stories, we realized that their journeys were not solely defined by how they moved through life as women, Black people, or mothers, but as a sum of all parts involved. Their identities as women of a certain age who grew up at a time when silence was golden, intersected with their responsibilities as Black mothers to shed that silence for the sake of their children.

On Multicultural Applicability

While our research focuses generally on duoethnography, we more specifically sought to better explain how we as Black women utilize the methods with our research on and with other Black women. However, we also consider what it means for other cultural, racial, and ethnic groups to perform similar research within their own in-groups.

First, when doing this research with other cultural groups, using culturally relevant artifacts and methodologies that resonate with the community's lived experiences is essential and invaluable. Methods such as *photovoice*, which allows participants to express their perspectives through photography, and *narrative inquiry*, which focuses on storytelling as a form of knowledge, provide powerful tools to center participants' voices (Wang & Burris, 1997; Connelly & Clandinin, 1990). These approaches not only allow for more inclusive and authentic data collection but also enable participants to communicate their experiences in meaningful, culturally resonant ways, disrupting traditional academic methods and expanding what is considered valid knowledge (Garrett et al., 2024; Teasdell et al., 2021).

In this way, research with other cultural groups should prioritize culturally relevant methods that challenge the conventional boundaries of knowledge production (Brown, 2024). By disrupting the foundation and historical contexts of academic research, scholars can create more inclusive, innovative, and impactful scholarship that will resonate both within academia and in the broader communities it aims to serve. This shift will impact academia by transforming how we understand, value, and engage with diverse forms of knowledge, contributing to a richer, more equitable landscape (Keikelame & Swartz, 2019). We encourage scholars to do similar work and make similar considerations as we transform the field with different ontological and epistemological truths found in our cultural celebrations, traditions, and knowing.

Suggestions for Further Reading and References

Ashlee, A. A., & Quaye, S. J. (2021). On being racially enough: A duoethnography across minoritized racial identities. *International Journal of Qualitative Studies in Education, 34*(3), 243–261. https://doi.org/10.1080/09518398.2020.1753256

Breault, R. A. (2016). Emerging issues in duoethnography. *International Journal of Qualitative Studies in Education, 29*(6), 777–794. https://doi.org/10.1080/09518398.2016.1162866

Brigance, C. A., & Brigance, M. L. (2023). A qualitative study of a couple experiencing reproductive trauma: An attachment perspective through a duoethnography. *Journal of Couple & Relationship Therapy, 22*(2), 105–129.

Brown, A. L. (2024). *Triumphantly taking tenure: Reflections of Black women faculty in higher education* [Doctoral dissertation, Wayne State University]. https://www.proquest.com/docview/3069018136/abstract/F65E7C3F65704440PQ/1

Brown, K. J., & Gilbert, L. M. (2021). Black hair as metaphor explored through duoethnography and arts-based research. *Journal of Folklore and Education, 8*, 85–106.

Burleigh, D., & Burm, S. (2022). Doing duoethnography: Addressing essential methodological questions. *International Journal of Qualitative Methods, 21*. 1–8. https://doi.org/10.1177/16094069221140876

Connelly, F. M., & Clandinin, D. J. (1990). Stories of experience and narrative inquiry. *Educational Researcher, 19*(5), 2–14. https://doi.org/10.3102/0013189X019005002

Council on Social Work Education. (2020). *2020 strategic plan*. https://www.cswe.org/about-cswe/2020-strategic-plan/

Garrett, R., Taylor, M. D., & Brown, A. L. (2024, April 12). *Prestige or peril: Experiences of Black doctoral students at a predominately white institution* [Paper presentation]. American Educational Research Association, Philadelphia, PA.

Gitterman, A. (2014). Social work: A profession in search of its identity. *Journal of Social Work Education, 50*(4), 599–607. https://doi.org/10.1080/10437797.2014.947898

Houston, W., & Winans, C. (1996). *Count on me* [Song]. On *Waiting to exhale: Original soundtrack album*. Arista Records.

Johnson, L. S. (2015). *Using sista circles to examine the professional experience of contemporary Black women teachers in schools: A collective story about school culture and support* [Doctoral dissertation]. University of Georgia.

Karas, M., & Uchihara, T. (2021). Silence: A duoethnography. *Journal of Silence Studies in Education, 1*(1), 64–75. https://doi.org/10.31763/jsse.v1i1.

Keikelame, M. J., & Swartz, L. (2019). Decolonising research methodologies: Lessons from a qualitative research project, Cape Town, South Africa. *Global Health Action, 12*(1), 1561175. https://doi.org/10.1080/16549716.2018.1561175

Koonce, J., & Lewis, K. (2020). Culturally relevant care through the lens of duoethnography. *The Qualitative Report, 25*(6), 1721–1735. https://doi.org/10.46743/2160-3715/2020.4489

Latz, A. O., & Murray, J. L. (2012). A duoethnography on duoethnography: More than a book review. *The Qualitative Report, 17*(36), 1–8.

Merleau-Ponty, M., & Smith, C. (1962). *Phenomenology of perception* (Vol. 26). Routledge.

Norris, J., & Sawyer, R. D. (2004). Null and hidden curricula of sexual orientation: A dialogue on the curreres of the absent presence and the present absence. In L. Coia, N. J. Brooks, S. J. Mayer, P. Pritchard, E. Heilman, M. L. Birch, & A. Mountain (Eds.), *Democratic responses in an era of standardization* (pp. 139–159). Curriculum and Pedagogy.

Sawyer, R. D., & Norris, J. (2009). *Duoethnography*. Brill.

Sawyer, R. D., & Norris, J. (2013). *Duoethnography*. Oxford University Press.

Sawyer, R. D., & Norris, J. (2016). Dialogic interdisciplinary self-study through the practice of duoethnography. In R. D. Sawyer & J. Norris (Eds.), *Interdisciplinary reflective practice through duoethnography: Examples for educators* (pp. 1–13). Palgrave Macmillan

Shelton, N. R. & McDermott, M. (2012). A curriculum of beauty. In J. Norris, R. D. Sawyer & D. Lund (Eds.), *Duoethnography: Dialogic methods for social, health, and educational research* (pp. 223–242). Left Coast.

Sions, H. K., & Coleman, A. C. (2019). "The team is all White": Reflections of art educators of color on Whiteness. *Journal of Cultural Research in Art Education, 36*(1), 29–55.

Teasdell, A., Lee, S. J., Calloway, A. M., & Adams, T. R. (2021). Commitment, community and consciousness: A collaborative autoethnography of a doctoral sister circle. *Journal of African American Women and Girls in Education, 1*(1). 7–23.

Thomas, N., & Blanc, V. (2021). Break it then build again: An arts based duoethnographic pilot reconstructing music therapy and dance/movement therapy histories. *The arts in Psychotherapy, 73*, 101765.

Wang, C., & Burris, M. A. (1997). Photovoice: Concept, methodology, and use for participatory needs assessment. *Health Education & Behavior, 24*(3), 369–387. https://doi.org/10.1177/109019819702400309

West, N. M., Payne, A. N., Smith, M. D., Bonds, N. T., Alston, A. D., & Akalugwu, W. N. (2021). A collaborative autoethnography of six Black women walking tightropes in higher education. *Negro Educational Review, 72*(1–4), 131–163.

Wilson, G. J., & Shields, S. S. (2019). Troubling the "WE" in art education: Slam poetry as subversive duoethnography. *Journal of Social Theory in Art Education, 39*(1), 6–18.

Winfield, A. S., Hickerson, H., Doub, D. C., Winfield, A. R., & McPhatter, B. (2024). Between Black mothers and daughters: A critical intergenerational duoethnography on the silence of health disparities and hope of loud healing. *Frontiers in Communication, 8*. 1–21. https://doi.org/10.3389/fcomm.2023.1185919

Woods, G. H., Pete, M. J., & Almánzar, B. (2024). *Wanna be (Remix)* [Song]. Collective Music Group; Interscope Records.

Chapter 7 Discussion Questions

1. How does duoethnography challenge traditional epistemological frameworks in academia? Reflect on how this method amplifies marginalized voices and critiques the hierarchical structures of knowledge production. What implications might this have for broader institutional change?
2. The authors emphasize the importance of trust and vulnerability in the duoethnographic process, particularly in their work with Black mothers. How do these elements influence the research outcomes and relationships among participants? In what ways might this emphasis on relationality be applied to other qualitative research methods?
3. Duoethnography is presented as both a methodology and an epistemological stance. How might this method be adapted to address systemic inequalities in other interdisciplinary fields, such as social work, public health, or education? Provide examples of how its tenets might enhance research in these areas.
4. Discuss the role of storytelling in duoethnography as a tool for social justice. How does centering personal narratives disrupt systemic oppression and empower participants? What are some potential challenges or criticisms of relying on storytelling as a primary mode of inquiry in academic research? How might these be addressed?

EIGHT

Photovoice in Critical Qualitative Research

Tim Monreal

What is Photovoice? A Broad View

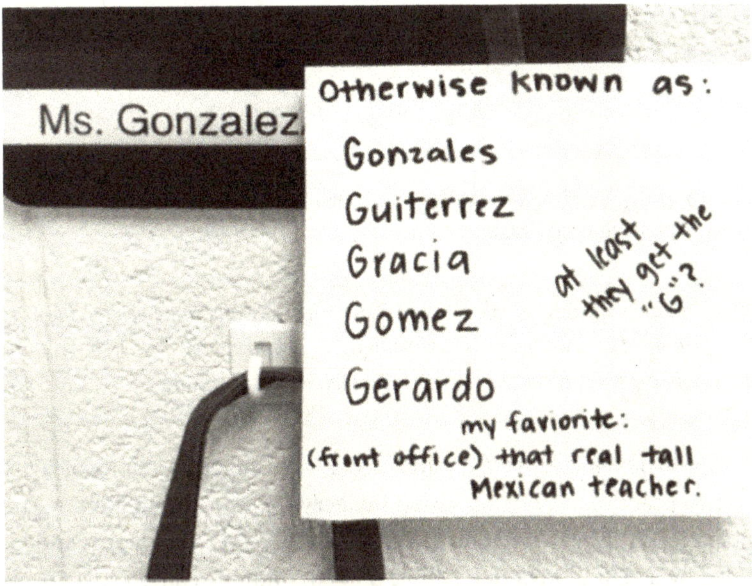

Figure 8.1. Image and (below) narrative from a photovoice study that the author led in October 2019.

> *Cause I always get it, whether it's in a [parent] note or it's up in the front office where they're like, I'm here to see miss blah, blah, blah. And my poor secretary has tried to figure out who they are talking, talking about . . . Um, yeah, so that's been here for the first nine weeks. Those are the names I've gotten . . .*
>
> *"the real tall Mexican teacher" is my favorite.*

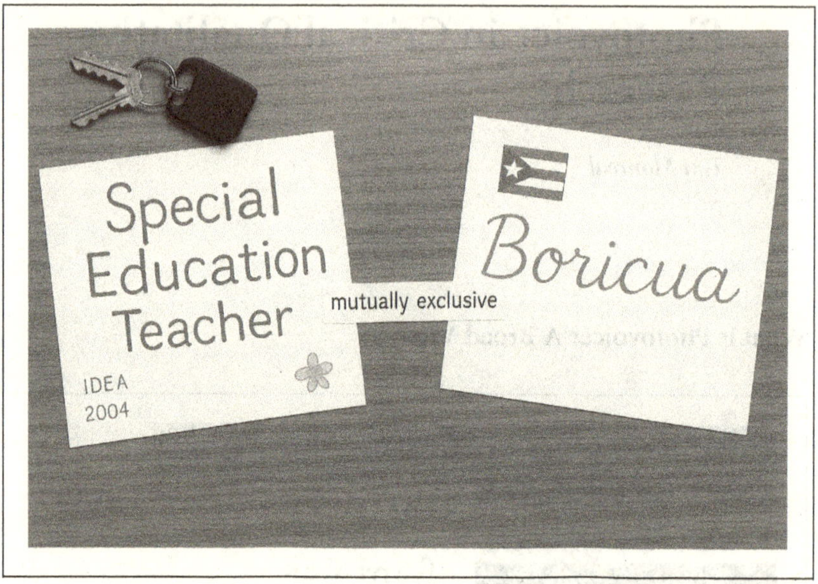

Figure 8.2. Image and (below) narrative from a photovoice study that the author led in October 2019. Reproduced image.

> *Those are two different people . . . even though it's the exact same person, the exact same name, those two are seen so differently. . . . It's like, they have to be separate. It's just like, they can't be the same. . . . You know what I mean?*

AT A MOST BASIC LEVEL, and as the word suggests, photovoice brings two practices—creating visual imagery (*photo*) and creating narrative explanations (*voice*)—together to center participants' own words and ideas. Guided by a central idea that people and communities have expertise about the social factors influencing their own lives, Latz (2017), echoing Wang and Burris' (1997) original articulation of photovoice (PV), described three common aims for using the method: a) to encourage participants to document elements of their lives within their own terms, b) to raise levels of critical consciousness through critical dialogue, and c) to reach policymakers with project findings to catalyze change (p. 43). Toward these ends, PV focuses the camera (increasingly a cell phone camera) as a crucial tool for participants to document, make sense of, and respond to guiding prompts and/or a specific topic. A paramount partner to these photographs is the way the participants choose words to provide insight into *everyday* practices, phenomena, and issues. Said another way, Annang et al. (2016a) described PV as a qualitative method of inquiry that evidences the power of photos and dialogues to understand "the cultural practices and lived experiences of individuals and communities" (p. 243) while also providing participants' own evidence and ideas for meaningful change.

The chapter's opening images and quotations provide a broad view of PV in practice. The pictures and text that begin this section are from a larger study (Monreal, 2020, 2022a) where I worked with Latinx[1] K–12 public school teachers in South Carolina. For the PV portion of the research project, participants took photos in response to the following prompt: *What images best communicate your experiences as a Latinx teacher in South Carolina?* The images, paired with accompanying dialogue from a semi-structured interview, are from one participant, an elementary special education teacher named "Mary." Mary shared how the general public struggled to imagine, perhaps even accept, the possibility of a Puerto Rican special education teacher. Mary explained how parents, community members, and staff assumed that as a Latina teacher, she *must* be Mexican and a Spanish teacher, and that as a special education teacher, she *must not* be Puerto Rican. Given the severe lack of Latinx teachers in a state (South Carolina) with a rapidly growing Latinx population, I chose PV as a way to highlight and learn from the knowledge of those closest to the problem of teacher representation. Like Mary, the participants in the study shared their experiences in a visceral manner, offering a praxis of *critical hope* that critiqued racist school policies and workplaces while also sharing individual acts of resistance and success (see Monreal & Floyd, 2021).

Doing Photovoice

Maxwell (2013) notes that there is no *cookbook* for doing qualitative research, and thus, this more detailed look at doing PV is more of a guide, a peek into the *black box* (Shah, 2105) of this dynamic method. In her book *Photovoice Research in Education*, Latz (2017) outlined eight steps for a PV methodology. While these steps are neither authoritative nor static, they provide a roadmap for researchers to think and plan alongside. I encourage interested researchers to engage with Latz's text (and some of the other foundational resources that come near the end of the chapter), but I now share some general points and examples using the eight-step framework.

1. Identification

Identifying the reasons behind and hopes for a project are important. In particular, I have found Maxwell's (2013) suggestion to work through a triad of goals—personal, practical, and intellectual—to be most helpful in this accord. In PV, researchers may want to identify a topic and/or issue and the groups of people who have firsthand experience with it. As a type of participatory method, PV researchers should think about how and when they will partner, even plan, with participants. Part of this beginning work might also include identifying whom to share the findings with and how the findings might be used to influence policy (-makers).

2. Invitation and 3. Education

Latz (2017) lists these steps separately, but I chose to combine the two because, in my previous experience with PV, the ask for and consent of participation requires an understanding of what the participants will do (PV education). In my research using PV (see Monreal, 2020), I often scheduled one or two informal chats or *cafecitos* with potential participants to build rapport and trust. As part of these conversations, I discussed the larger project and gauged their general interest. I then shared a presentation that discussed PV, showed examples of photos, and went over ethics. Generally, the more participatory the design and planning of the PV project, the more these first steps will overlap; sometimes, this participatory nature is imperative when working with groups and communities that have been the targets rather than beneficiaries of research (for examples, see Allen & Hutchinson, 2009 and Castleden et al., 2008).

4. Documentation

This phase involves the actual creation of photographs. Latz (2017) maintains that effective prompts are most vital to navigating this phase and aligning the responses with research aims. Prompts should be open-ended but can focus on a single question, center a general theme, fill in a blank, follow a directive statement, and/or complete a phrase. Latz shared a few examples, including "What do you like best about school," "Show what diversity means to you," and "Mathematics is . . ." (p. 71). Using a slightly different approach, de los Ríos (2017, see also 2020) had students take photographs of "their understandings of ethnic studies, themselves, and their communities in relation to colonialism, hegemony, and racism" (p. 17) over the span of four months. Students dropped photos into an online Google folder. This step may also be part of the education phase as researchers decide whether or not the degree of guidance, modeling, and/or coaching is appropriate.

5. *Narration*

The photo itself is not *the* data: The data is created in conversation with the participant. As Latz stated, "it is not the researcher's role to interpret these photos. That is the domain of the participants" (p. 74). Most often, dialogue is driven through an interview; options include open-ended, semi-structured, and focus groups. Latz recommended four general parts to a PV interview: a) warm-up questions, b) photo elucidation, c) process questions, and d) additional information such as demographic (as needed). Another way of guiding the interview is with the acronym SHOWeD. In their PV research, Annang Ingram et al. (2016a) and Goessling (2018) explain how they asked participants: a) What did they **See** happening?; b) What is *really* **Happening**?; c) How does this relate to **Our** lives?; d) **Why** do these experiences and issues exist?; and e) What can we **Do** about it? In my research using PV, participants liked knowing we would use a structure like SHOWeD, even as the interviews often became informal and conversational. Other discursive strategies might include having participants caption photos, create voice memos/recordings, or rank the images.

6. *Analysis*

Latz named this sixth step *ideation* because it can, maybe even should, be a participatory process that produces knowledge *and* identifies action steps toward representation and/or change. Producing knowledge may include customary qualitative processes of organizing and coding the data toward the creation of themes. In a more grounded theory approach, researchers and participants may also think with and/or aim to create their own theories oriented at explaining, making sense of, or creating change. Analysis may also include how the group and participants believe the data can help make change. This may include selecting certain photographs and highlighting particular narratives as part of a public presentation or event (Wang & Burris, 1997). Equally of note is how the group may *refuse* to show and share certain pictures and knowledge (see also Del Vecchio et al., 2017).

7. Presentation and 8. Confirmation

A crucial part of PV is how the analysis and findings are (re)presented in ways that benefit the participants, community members, and academic researchers. Often, an important aim of PV is to highlight and create particular knowledges while also working to influence policy change. Thus, form presentations of PV research range from formal exhibitions to posters, presentations, brochures, open-access (journal) articles, and digital media. Given ever-evolving technological affordances, researchers and participants are incorporating tools like such as QR codes, social media, video, and augmented reality to create myriad presentations that exist beyond fixed notions of space and time. This also leans into the flexibility of PV, as research teams combine and entangle different methods and tools to serve myriad goals. For example, I combined PV with eco-mapping to engage and interact with teachers' spatial worlds (Monreal, 2022b), and Hidalgo (2015) used elements of PV to create augmented-reality *fotonovelas*. Finally, as photographs, stories, and presentations are affective mediums, they elicit different, sometimes visceral emotional responses. Hence, thinking of presentations as a site of inquiry into participant and attendee experience is a newer focus of research that Latz (see also, Mitchell et al., 2017, p. 98) names as *confirmation*.

In sum, PV (sometimes woven with other methods) provides entry points toward "new possibles" (Kuntz, 2019, p. 40), where participants and researchers inter (and intra-)act[2] with and value one another. The hope is that this type of engagement facilitates knowing *in and as* an action where different people come together to "map the *immediate now* towards productive fractures" (p. 16). (Re)asserting their/our/each other's/one another's agencies to be with/in the world, PV promotes research as developing participatory spaces of action

(Mitchell et al., 2017). It is precisely this idea of participatory work that helps disrupt systems of oppression.

Disrupting Systems of Oppression and Empowering Participants

Figure 8.3. Image and (next) narrative from a photovoice study that the author led in April 2022.

> *I mean some, some people that I meet at these parties [quinceañeras, baptismos, etc.], they have like this expectation of a teacher, you know, like "he doesn't drink," you know, "no eche relajo" and stuff. And then they see me, you know, drinking, you know, having a good time and everything, and then I tell them I'm a teacher, and they're like, "You're a teacher? Really?"*

PV research is rooted within a participatory research paradigm that outlines an experiential, propositional, practical, and co-created knowing of and being in the world (Lincoln et al., 2011). Significantly, many of the PV examples I reference throughout this chapter (e.g., de los Ríos, 2017, 2020;

Del Vecchio et al., 2017; Hidalgo, 2015; Latz, 2017; Wang & Burris, 1997) directly trace an understanding of participatory (and critical) visual methods to Freire's (1970) ubiquitous work in anti-oppressive and liberatory education. In this vein, PV, like education more broadly, is rooted in a dialogical process that is done *with* rather than for or on people. This requires a fundamentally different view of participants as meaningful collaborators and coinvestigators rather than objects of inquiry, recipients of aid, or variables to manipulate (Lake & Wendland, 2018). As Lincoln et al. (2011) write, "coresearchers are initiated into the inquiry process by a facilitator/researcher and learn through active engagement in the process" (p. 101). In a Freirean sense, focusing the knowledge and wisdom of people lies at the core of a problem- (ex)posing methodology that empowers participants to develop and cultivate critical examination of social injustice and structures of inequality.

This link to Freirean praxis—a commitment to both the theory and practice of social change—situates PV within the general auspice of Participatory Action Research (PAR). An emphasis on collaborative, participant-driven knowledge production necessarily disrupts a view of academic research that substitutes a narrow focus of apolitical, objective, and positivist methods for the messiness of transformative justice work. Kemmis and McTaggart (2008) offer three broad criteria to differentiate PAR from conventional research: shared ownership of research projects, community-based analysis of social problems, and an orientation toward community action. Similarly, Allen and Hutchinson (2009) understand PAR to be guided by general principles, including democratic participation in all (or often some) aspects of the research, equal power and equal respect for the knowledge domains of all participants, and particular attention to the needs of those who are marginalized. Lake and Wendland (2018) find that across disciplines and projects, PAR researchers "articulate a core commitment to social justice, ethical relationships with participants, democratic and inclusive practices, and altering unjust and inequitable systems" (p. 11). Thus, PV, situated within PAR, is a dynamic method to highlight how webs of power produce what counts as knowledge and why some knowledges (seem to) count more than others (Foucault, 1980). It is precisely the emphasis on critiquing traditional knowledge production, a process traditionally used as a tool for marginalization and colonization (Smith, 2012), that makes PV/PAR a tool to invite collaborative inquiry into inclusive, equitable, and just ways of *becoming* in the world.

I firmly believe this notion (and potential) of *becoming* is one that deserves greater attention in PV specifically and critical qualitative research more generally. Kuntz (2019) warns us that qualitative inquiry easily slips into a representational exercise as researchers seek to excavate a priori truths (inadvertently), normalizing the repetition of the status quo. As such, it is vital that researchers resist the framing of pictures (and dialogue) as representing a thing (out there) and instead opt for PV as a process, a critical inquiry into the multiplicitous sets of (power) relations that reveal "blurry edges to our known existence—spaces of potential that would otherwise remain just beyond recognition" (Kuntz, 2019, p. 2). PV research, seen as a processual and contested 'site' rather than a representational excavation, acknowledges the unequal relations of knowledge production and asserts the importance of critical methods that disrupt such relationships.

For example, the previous picture and dialogue are taken from a research project where I used PV to examine what it means to be/become a Latinx teacher in rural, conservative areas of South Carolina. In the photo and excerpt, we see how "Jaime," a middle school science teacher, *uses* PV to critique certain politics of representation that tie Latinx teachers to subject positions like 'proper' and 'well-behaved' role models. Resisting these discourses that seek to discipline his self-conduct, Jaime produces alternative ways of becoming a Latinx teacher, one in which you could be a good teacher *and* also have a good time (for an extended discussion of PV and the (re)construction of subject positions, see Monreal 2021, 2024). Jamie's articulation of his myriad Latinx teacher subjectivities provides entry points for him and others "to challenge, accept, antagonize, internalize, even ignore who, what, and where they are hailed to be" (Monreal, 2020, p. 12). This has policy implications, as programs that ephemerally call for individual Latinx teachers to *be* individual solutions to structural injustice rely on flattened views of innate correspondence that ignore the nuance and differences of Latinx teacher and educator *becoming*.

Foundational Texts and Important Theorists

Across the chapter, I have named important articles and thinkers as I sought to provide poignant examples of PV. However, at the risk of being repetitive, I share a bit more information about some of these scholars and texts. First, it is helpful to situate the lineage of such critical visual research methods. Freire's (1970) *Pedagogy of the Oppressed* provides a theoretical grounding and primary source of important terms and concepts that are quite common across PV research. Additionally, Freire's (1985) book *The Politics of Education: Culture, Power, and Liberation* is a helpful continuation for researchers and participants. Gubrium and Harper's (2013) book *Participatory Visual and Digital Methods* and Mitchell et al.'s (2017) text *Participatory Visual Methodologies: Social Change, Community, and Policy*, besides providing extensive showing of PV (and its entanglement with other methods), both discuss Freire's connection to the technique.

Other important theoretical foundations include Linda Tuhiwai Smith's (2012) indispensable classic *Decolonizing Methodologies: Research and Indigenous Peoples*. Del Vecchio et al. (2017) illuminate what Smith's ideas look like in their article that examines PV, place, and refusal with undocumented youth. In terms of building the praxis of PV, it is essential that researchers engage with Wang & Burris (1997) and Latz (2017). While I discuss Latz's work at length in the chapter, it is important to read her own book as she traces her own development and use of PV in conversation with Wang & Burris' seminal methodological work. I find the work of Annang Ingram et al. (2016a, b), Castleden et al. (2008), and Goessling (2018) to be helpful in thinking through participant and community relationships and rely on the work of de los Ríos (2017, 2020) and Hidalgo (2015) for melding creativity with criticality. Finally, I have shared many of my own publications where PV was a central method. In particular, my work puts PV in conversation with space (Monreal, 2024), Latinx Studies (Monreal, 2021), post-structuralism (Monreal, 2020, 2022a), and complementary techniques such as eco-mapping (Monreal, 2022b).

Notes

1. I use Latinx as an inclusive term that represents a spectrum of gender identity.

2. Intra-action is a neologism introduced by quantum physicist Karen Barad (2007) that attempts to capture the emergence of things, ideas, forces, and agencies through immanent, but unequal, relationships between non/living actors. Whereas any interaction takes place between two independent actors, intra-actions occur from within, when two or more entities become inseparable. This view is indispensable in my understanding of the *productive*, rather than representative functions of PV.

Suggestions for Further Reading and References

Allen, D., & Hutchinson, T. (2009). Using PAR or abusing its good name? The challenges and surprises of Photovoice and film in a study of chronic illness. *International Journal of Qualitative Methods, 8*(2), 115–128. https://doi.org/10.1177/160940690900800203

Annang Ingram, L., Tinago, C. B., Estrada, R., Wilson, S., Wright Sanders, L., Bevington, T., Carlos, B., Cornelius, E., Svendsen, E. R., & Ball, J. (2016a). Off the rails in rural South Carolina: A qualitative study of healthcare provider perspectives on the long-term health impact of the Graniteville train disaster. *Rural and Remote Health*. http://www.rrh.org.au/Articles/printviewnew.asp?ArticleID=3906

Annang Ingram, L., Wilson, S., Tinago, C., Wright Sanders, L., Bevington, T., Carlos, B., Cornelius, E., & Svendsen, E. (2016b). Photovoice: Assessing the long-term impact of a disaster on a community's quality of life. *Qualitative Health Research, 26*(2), 241–251.

Barad, K. (2007). *Meeting the universe halfway: Quantum Physics and the entanglement of matter and meaning*. Duke University Press.

Castleden, H., Garvin, T., & Huu-ay-aht First Nation, H. (2008). Modifying photovoice for community-based participatory Indigenous research. *Social Science & Medicine, 66*(6), 1393–1405. https://doi.org/10.1016/j.socscimed.2007.11.030

de los Ríos, C. V. (2017). Picturing ethnic studies: Photovoice and youth literacies of social action. *Journal of Adolescent & Adult Literacy, 61*(1), 15–24. https://doi.org/doi: 10.1002/jaal.631

de los Ríos, C. V. (2020). Writing oneself into the curriculum: Photovoice journaling in a secondary ethnic studies course. *Written Communication, 37*(4), 487–511. http://dx.doi.org/10.1177/0741088320938794

Del Vecchio, D., Toomey, N., & Tuck, E. (2017). Placing photovoice: Participatory action research with undocumented migrant youth in the Hudson Valley. *Critical Questions in Education, 8*(4), 358–376.

Foucault, M. (1980). *Power/Knowledge: Selected interviews and other writings, 1972-1977* (C. Gordon, Ed.). Vintage.

Freire, P. (1970). *Pedagogy of the oppressed*. Continuum.

Freire, P. (1985). *The politics of education: Culture, power, and liberation*. Bergin & Garvey.

Goessling, K. P. (2018). Increasing the depth of field: Critical race theory and photovoice as counter storytelling praxis. *The Urban Review, 50*(4), 648–674. https://doi.org/10.1007/s11256-018-0460-2

Gubrium, A., & Harper, K. (2013). *Participatory visual and digital methods*. Routledge.

Hidalgo, L. (2015). Augmented Fotonovelas: Creating new media as pedagogical and social Justice tools. *Qualitative Inquiry, 21*(3), 300–314. https://doi.org/10.1177/1077800414557831

Kemmis, S., & McTaggart, R. (2008). Participatory action research: Communicative actions and the public sphere. In N. K. Denzin & Y. S. Lincoln (Eds.), *Strategies of qualitative inquiry* (pp. 271–330). SAGE Publications.

Kuntz, A. M. (2019). *Qualitative inquiry, cartography, and the promise of material change*. Routledge.

Lake, D., & Wendland, J. (2018). Practical, epistemological, and ethical challenges of Participatory Action Research: A cross-disciplinary review of the literature. *Journal of Higher Education Outreach and Engagement, 22*(3), 11–42.

Latz, A. O. (2017). *Photovoice research in education and beyond: A practical guide from theory to exhibition.* Routledge.

Lincoln, Y. S., Lynham, S., & Guba, E. (2011). Paradigmatic controversies, contradictions, and emerging confluences. In N. K. Denzin & Y. S. Lincoln (Eds.), *The Sage Handbook of Qualitative Research* (4th ed., pp. 97–128). SAGE Publications.

Maxwell, J. A. (2013). *Qualitative research design: An interactive approach.* SAGE Publications.

Mitchell, C., De Lange, N., & Molestane, R. (2017). *Participatory visual methodologies: Social change, community, and policy.* SAGE Publications Ltd.

Monreal, T. (2020). *Hecho en South Carolina: K-12 Latinx educators made in, and remaking, El Sur Latinx* [Dissertation]. University of South Carolina.

Monreal, T. (2021). Stitching together more expansive Latinx teacher self/ves: Movidas of Rasquache and spaces of counter-conduct in El Sur Latinx. *Theory, Research, and Action in Urban Education, 6*(1), 37–51.

Monreal, T. (2022a). "Here being in schools is worse": How Latinx teachers navigate, recreate, and instigate hostile spaces in the US South. *Educational Studies, 58*(1), 50–73. https://doi.org/10.1080/00131946.2021.1994972

Monreal, T. (2022b). "I feel like I am in-between. I am not from here or there. I don't belong": Using ecomaps to investigate the relational spaces of Latinx im/migrant teachers in South Carolina. In C. Magno, J. Lew, & S. Rodriguez (Eds.), *(Re)Mapping migration and education: Methods, theory, and practice.* (pp. 13–37). Brill.

Monreal, T. (2024). "No me dejaran ir porque they needed me here": Spatializing corrective representatives by critiquing Latinx teacher role model discourse. *Race Ethnicity and Education,* 1–20. https://doi.org/10.1080/13613324.2024.2306413

Monreal, T., & Floyd, R. (2021). "Ain't no white people have to be cultural ambassadors, right?" How a Latinx teacher in the US South resists ephemeral multiculturalism for political praxis. *Theory Into Practice, 60*(4), 412–421. https://doi.org/10.1080/00405841.2021.1987095

Shah, P. (2015). Spaces to speak: Photovoice and the reimagination of girls' education in India. *Comparative Education Review, 59*(1), 50–74. https://doi.org/10.1086/678699

Smith, L. T. (2012). *Decolonizing methodologies: Research and Indigenous peoples.* Zed Books.

Wang, C., & Burris, M. A. (1997). Photovoice: Concept, methodology, and use for participatory needs assessment. *Health Education and Behavior, 24*(3), 369–387. https://doi.org/10.1177/109019819702400309

Chapter 8 Discussion Questions

1. How does the concept of *photovoice* (PV) challenge traditional power dynamics between researchers and participants, and what role does participant-driven knowledge production play in this process?
2. Considering Latz's four parts of a PV interview, how can each stage (warm-up, photo elucidation, process questions, additional information) contribute to the development of a deeper understanding of the participants' lived experiences, particularly in relation to their social context?
3. How do the different components of a photovoice interview—warm-up questions, photo elucidation, and process questions—support participants in reflecting on and articulating their lived experiences, and how might this process foster a deeper understanding of social issues and potential for change?
4. How does the use of photovoice as a participatory method within the framework of Participatory Action Research (PAR) disrupt systems of oppression and offer a space for marginalized voices to challenge traditional notions of knowledge production?

NINE

Beyond a Research Tool: Faith Sharing as a Disruptive Qualitative Method

Christopher B. Tran

I FIRST UTILIZED FAITH SHARING AS a qualitative research method for my dissertation titled *Visit the Imprisoned: A Heuristic Inquiry into the Experiences of Catholic Detention Ministry Volunteers* (Tran, 2024). I reference my study throughout this chapter. Just like my dissertation, in an attempt to reduce the traditional power imbalance between the researcher and participant, I use the term *collaborator* whenever discussing research participants. Upon completion of my dissertation, I reflected on how I arrived at incorporating my personal faith with my research endeavor, as this was not common in academia. It was important to acknowledge that as a qualitative researcher grounded within a critical paradigm, I claimed my subjectivity as a vital tool in guiding my study. I drew upon my personal experiences as a Catholic detention ministry volunteer when interpreting and curating meaning from the study's findings. Therefore, not only did I desire for my dissertation to work towards humanization, but I also sought a nontraditional yet humanizing approach that disrupted conventional research methodologies.

Simply defined, faith sharing is a dialogical activity or practice where "each person offers their experiences of God's activity in their lives, perhaps where they felt most moved, or noticed God's presence" (Martin, 2019, para. 2). Essentially, faith sharing allows for personal reflection and collective dialogue upon an encounter between one's lived experiences and personal spirituality, or God. Although "faith" may possess different meanings and definitions, I refer to this notion as "the personal relationship and commitment a person has to God" (Schmitz, 2018, para. 4). Therefore, the intention of faith sharing as a practice is to share one's spiritual relationship to others within a collective space. When defining faith sharing and understanding it within the context of educational research methods, I specifically pull from an intersection of my Catholic understanding and the tenets of dialogue discussed by Paulo Freire (2018). In composing this chapter, I caution that faith sharing cannot and should not be merely reduced to a research method. Again, the intention of this practice involves the spiritual nature of humans, and its significance to individuals and religious groups should be respected. Rather than thinking of faith sharing as a data collection tool, I encourage researchers to utilize this method as an extension of their own innate spirituality that seeks to authentically explore and understand the human phenomenon at hand.

Faith sharing requires a space and opportunity for deep listening and understanding of the topic of inquiry. Within a research-methods context, faith sharing can resemble individual interviews or focus groups. Because in-depth interviewing is the primary method used in qualitative research studies (Marshall et al., 2022), I believed that faith sharing fit within my dissertation's methodology. Opposed to a highly structured design, I conducted informal, conversational *interviews* (Patton, 2015) for my study. I ultimately decided to use faith sharings as individual interviews because the conversations held within each sharing truly allowed the collaborators to share their faith experiences and reflect on their praxis of serving. This was also relevant to the topic of inquiry—exploring the experiences of Catholic detention ministry volunteers. When utilized as a research method, faith sharing may also incorporate other spiritual practices such as prayer, meditations, and rituals specific to the religion at hand. For instance, within my dissertation process, I began each faith sharing session with an invitation to prayer and concluded with a prayer as well.

Because faith sharing requires a level of vulnerability, researchers who pursue this method should consider the time and relationship it takes for collaborators to feel comfortable in order to share their personal experiences. When it comes to data collection, the sharing of one's experiences tied to their faith offers a rich conversation that elicits emotional, reflective insights from the collaborators. In my dissertation, I adopted Seidman's (2019) phenomenological interviewing approach, which consisted of three in-depth interviews with each collaborator. Conducting three faith sharing sessions with each individual allowed for a richer connection between myself (the researcher) and each collaborator. This meaningful relationship was important when creating a safe space for authentic dialogue and conversation. When considering the reflective aspect of this method, I gave each collaborator some time to reflect on their thoughts and experiences prior to coming to the faith sharing: approximately three to seven days prior to each session, I shared the interview questions (reflection questions) with each individual. I reminded the collaborators that these questions were to help guide the dialogue and that each session would be informal and conversational.

Specific to my study, each faith sharing lasted approximately 50 to 70 minutes, but this was not a prescribed time limit. Additionally, the three faith sharings with each collaborator were primarily spaced out from one week to one month between sessions, depending on the availability of myself and each person. Although I had the option for teleconferencing, I chose to conduct each faith sharing in person because I valued the importance of physical presence when sharing personal experiences. Deviating from Seidman's (2019) themes of his three interviews, I focused on concepts relating to my topic of inquiry. The first faith sharing focused on getting to know each volunteer's background and motivation for serving in detention ministry. The second faith sharing focused more on the specific experiences of directly serving those who were incarcerated. The last faith sharing focused on the volunteers' perceptions of the prison system and their call to action in regard to any perceived injustices surrounding incarceration. Choosing this method makes the most sense if the collaborators are grounded in their faith. Therefore, the researcher must acknowledge the spirituality embedded throughout their experiences. This means that the analysis and thematic explication processes would inevitably include faith and spiritual notions as well.

When thinking about utilizing faith sharing as a research method, the researcher should consider certain things. First, researchers should possess a deeply felt connection to the faith or spirituality at hand: This allows for an authentic approach to gathering information and making sense of what is explored and learned. The researcher should also have some prior experience engaging in faith sharings. Although I remained specifically within the Catholic faith, I acknowledge that other religions have their own forms of faith sharing, and I encourage researchers of different faiths to explore this method if desired and appropriate. Next, when deciding on a topic of inquiry for qualitative research, it is important to consider matching the appropriate methods to what is being examined. Faith sharings, in particular, can lend well to any topics relating to human experiences or thoughts where spirituality plays a mediating role. It can also be fitting if the collaborators closely identify with their faith. Finally, because this method requires an openness and vulnerability, it is important for the researcher to consider the potential for deeper and meaningful relationships formed with their collaborators, highlighting a *studying with* rather than a *studying on* spirit of research. Again, I want to reiterate the importance that faith sharing should not be reduced to merely a data collection tool: To authentically explore and deeply engage in the inquiry process, researchers who seek to use this method must themselves embrace and practice faith sharing as a means of their own spiritual motivations and discernment.

Disrupting Systems of Oppression and Empowering Participants

When examining the context for academia and research, nontraditional methods that utilize a more critical and humanizing approach ultimately disrupt conventional ways of learning and knowing. Broadly speaking, there is a positivist-quantitative hold over academia (universities, scholarly journals, other academic institutions, etc.) that prioritizes and pressures scholars to constantly produce research in order to maintain status and increase distinction. This *publish-or-perish* (Colquhoun, 2011) culture within the academy has led to ethical lapses such as research misconduct and breaches in institutional ethics (Heyneman, 2011). Moreover, it is important to acknowledge how research has historically been a colonizing practice (Smith, 2000) that has roots in the abuse and exploitation of vulnerable populations (von Engelhardt, 2007; Emanuel et al., 2003).

When I ultimately decided to utilize faith sharing as a research method within my dissertation, I acknowledged that this was not common and that incorporating spirituality or religiosity was scant in the literature. This was not the gold standard that I had been so conditioned to learn during my graduate studies, and I feared that it would be looked down upon. Despite these hesitations, engaging in faith sharings with my collaborators yielded rich testimonies and reflections that I did not believe could be gathered without it. In addition, through the lens of my faith, I valued the research journey—the rigor, trustworthiness, and goodness (Lincoln & Guba, 1985)—even more when I incorporated my spirituality in the process. Mogra (2017) discussed how researchers who leaned into their faith and spirituality during the research process ultimately practiced an added layer of protection and integrity. These researchers demonstrated an "alignment between ethics from the perspective of being a professional engaged in educational research with a personal significance based on one's belief, which takes a holistic notion of life . . . [with] an added dimension of being accountable to God" (Mogra, 2017, p. 365). Therefore, if researchers are truly authentic to the goodness of their religious beliefs and are sensitive to the ethical dimensions of the practice, ideally, they should minimize or avoid any oppressive methodologies.

Considering my own subjectivity and theoretical orientation, I sought a methodology that was humanizing in its approach and was respectful to all those who participated in my study. When it comes to gathering data, researchers need to be mindful of power dynamics within a conversation. They ought to establish or work towards an egalitarian relationship. Asymmetrical relationships (Sandstrom et al., 2006; Kvale, 2002) may have one party or individual imposing dominance over the other, and this is often true between the researcher and research participants. Privilege and oppression are deeply embodied experiences (Johnson, 2015) that are oftentimes unconscious or not realized until one intentionally engages in reflexivity to develop a self-awareness of one's position of power. The practice of faith sharing allows for reflexivity and vulnerability for all those involved. By engaging in the humble practice of sharing one's interior experiences and reflections, researchers can inevitably lessen power differences between them and their collaborators.

For my dissertation, because my collaborators possessed a spiritual and religious identity, faith sharing ultimately served as a culturally responsive research method (Berryman et al., 2013) that honored the ways in which my collaborators understood their experiences. By utilizing a shared and familiar practice, I was able to accompany my collaborators on a research journey to genuinely explore their experiences. This practice essentially worked against traditional data collecting methods where the intention was to gather information without respect to where or who it came from. From my experiences, faith sharings allowed for a common language and helped lower barriers between sharing personal experiences. Moreover, through each meeting, my collaborators and I formed a special connection, truly as "brothers and sisters" in Christ (New American Bible, Revised Edition, 2011). Through this relationship, I witnessed how my collaborators comfortably spoke with an openness, not needing to say the correct answer or impress me as the researcher. I can affirm the veracity of their responses because I also utilized member-checking (Lincoln & Guba, 1985; Rolfe, 2006) in order to clarify anything that was stated during the faith sharings and to validate the interpretation of their words. I found that through the method of faith sharing and the incorporation of a shared spiritual identity, each collaborator was empowered to authentically share their truth and experiences without the concern of manipulation or exploitation.

Foundational Texts and Important Theorists

When I first began my dissertation process, I did not initially foresee myself using faith sharing as a data collection method, nor did I think it would be possible. In my review of the literature, I did not find any study utilizing this method. In regard to developing this technique, I eventually came to the faith sharing method by allowing my research journey to guide me. Given the various qualitative methodological designs, I picked the methodology that best approached my topic of inquiry as well as my relationship to the phenomenon. Because I sought to authentically explore the experiences of Catholic detention ministry volunteers, and because I also identified as one myself, I opted to utilize heuristic inquiry (Moustakas, 1961; Sultan, 2018), which stemmed from the broader methodology of phenomenology.

In general, phenomenology invites people to deeply engage with the experiences at hand to "make sense of them directly and immediately" (Crotty, 1998, p. 79) with the potential of discovering new meaning. In this design, the researcher ultimately becomes an instrument who explores, analyzes, and transforms the collaborators' spoken experiences in hopes of capturing the essential features of the human phenomenon. Specifically, heuristic inquiry seeks to understand the specific phenomenon through exploring the relationship between the individual and their experience (Sultan, 2018). More nuanced than broader phenomenology, researchers who use a heuristic research design possess a surely felt interest or a shared connection to the experience that influences their decision to further explore the topic (Moustakas, 1961). Therefore, what a heuristic researcher senses, feels, and thinks about certain phenomena are instrumental and considered during the research journey.

> [Heuristic Inquiry] creates a space for the magic that happens when researcher and co-researchers come together in shared curiosity and open ourselves up to

> becoming enchanted and transformed, not only by findings embedded in real-life experience but by the pull of the process itself on our souls. (Sultan, 2018, p. 22)

In regards to my dissertation, not only did I share in the experience of volunteering in detention ministry, but I also shared the same faith identity of being Catholic. Keeping this in mind, I was drawn back to my own spiritual practices and reflected on how I came to understand my spirituality and my ministry experiences. Therefore, by fully immersing myself in the heuristic research process, I was led to discover that faith sharing was the common language that allowed me to garner rich dialogue and the elicitation of experiences from my collaborators. Moreover, this practice profoundly resonated with my collaborators, who were people of faith.

In addition to being guided by the methodological design, my personal motivations for pursuing my doctoral research were ultimately grounded within educational and spiritual frameworks such as Critical Pedagogy (Freire, 2018) and Liberation Theology (Gutiérrez, 1973). Not only did these frameworks guide a sociopolitical analysis of the prison and incarceration context, but they fostered my desire to utilize research to help build a socially just world by centering the lives of the oppressed and challenging me to see how God might want me to see: a world in need of greater love and solidarity.

When specifically conceptualizing faith sharings, I draw from Critical Pedagogy and Freire's (2018) tenets for authentic dialogue: love, humility, and faith. Earlier, I mentioned that faith sharings resemble individual interviews or focus groups with an added dimension of spirituality. In order for researchers to partake in a vibrant exchange of ideas, reflections, cultural memories, and experiences, it is important to note that these conversations must adopt an aspect of authentic dialogue. First, these faith sharing sessions must be grounded in a "profound love for the world and for people. . . . Love is at the same time the foundation of dialogue and dialogue itself" (Freire, 2018, p. 89). The researcher must embrace and exude a tender love during each encounter with their research collaborators.

Additionally, Freire (2005) asserted that authentic dialogue can occur only when the dialoguers possessed humility, which he described as requiring "courage, self-confidence, self-respect, and respect for others" (p. 72). By embracing humility, the researcher can then become open to the potential for personal transformation, a "changing of consciousness" (Freire, 1985, p. 123), and "a conversion to the people" (Freire, 2018, p. 61). Finally, Freire discussed the necessity of faith: "Dialogue further requires an intense faith in humankind, faith in their power to make and remake, to create and re-create, faith in their vocation to be more fully human" (Freire, 2018, p. 90). Freire (2018) warned that "without this faith in people, dialogue is a farce which inevitably degenerates into paternalistic manipulation" (p. 91), in which the researcher may perpetuate "the oppressor housed within" (Freire, 2018, p. 135). Without an understanding of Freirean dialogue, this technique may shy away from being a method that disrupts traditional systems of oppression. Therefore, I encourage researchers who yearn to utilize faith sharing as a data collection method to be mindful of the characteristics needed for these intimate, critical, and transformative conversations.

To conclude, I carried fear and anxiety as a novice researcher to conduct what I wanted as the most perfect study. Most of my undergraduate and graduate exposure to research revolved around quantitative approaches that represented the gold standard of practice. Deciding to utilize a qualitative design for my dissertation was a departure from the rigidity of traditional research. This decision did not come without hesitation and doubts, but looking back, I do not regret it. Coming from a constructionist epistemology, I became open to the different and vast ways of knowing. I had to look inward and trust my intuition and reflexivity throughout the research journey.

Moreover, I grounded myself in educational and theoretical frameworks that guided me through an active and reflective praxis. With prayer, reflection, and allowing the Spirit to move me, I learned so much from my dissertation journey. My encouragement to fellow researchers is to ground oneself in the values of working towards a more loving and socially just world. From there, I urge researchers to break away from traditional ways of knowing and practice in order to disrupt the hegemony of academia. Through prioritizing ethical and humanizing approaches that respect and uplift humanity, research can become a beacon for both personal and collective transformation.

Suggestions for Further Reading and References

Berryman, M., SooHoo, S., & Nevin, A. (2013). *Culturally responsive methodologies from the margins*. Emerald Group Publishing.

Colquhoun, D. (2011, September 5). *Publish-or-perish: Peer review and the corruption of science.* The Guardian. https://www.theguardian.com/science/2011/sep/05/publish-perish-peer-review-science

Crotty, M. (1998). *The foundations of social research: Meaning and perspective in the research process.* SAGE.

Emanuel, E. J., Crouch, R. A., Arras, J. D., Moreno, J. D., & Grady, C. (2003). Scandals and tragedies of research with human participants. In E. J. Emanuel, R. A. Crouch, J. D. Arras, J. D. Moreno, & C. Grady (Eds.), *Ethical and regulatory aspects of clinical research* (pp. 1–5). John Hopkins University Press.

Freire, P. (1985). *The politics of education: Culture, power, and liberation.* Bergin & Garvey.

Freire, P. (2005). *Teachers as cultural workers: Letters to those who dare teach* (expanded edition). Westview Press.

Freire, P. (2018). *Pedagogy of the oppressed.* Bloomsbury Publishing.

Gutiérrez, G. (1973). *A theology of liberation: History, politics, and salvation.* Orbis Books.

Heyneman, S. P. (2011). The corruption of ethics in higher education. *International Higher Education, 62*, 8–9. https://doi.org/10.6017/ihe.2011.62.8530

Johnson, R. (2015). Grasping and transforming the embodied experience of oppression. *International Body Psychotherapy Journal, 14*(1), 80–95.

Kvale, S. (2002). *Dialogue as oppression and interview research.* Paper presented at the Nordic Educational Research Association Conference. Tallinn, Estonia.

Lincoln, Y. S., & Guba, E. (1985). *Naturalistic inquiry.* SAGE.

Marshall, C., Rossman, G. B., & Blanco, G. L. (2022). *Designing qualitative research* (7th ed.). SAGE.

Martin, J. (2019, July 22). *How faith sharing can benefit your spiritual life. America: The Jesuit Review.* https://www.americamagazine.org/faith/2019/07/22/how-faith-sharing-can-benefit-your-spiritual-life

Mogra, I. (2017). Strengthening ethics: A faith perspective on educational research. *Journal of Academic Ethics, 15*(4), 365–376. https://doi.org/10.1007/s10805-017-9292-z

Moustakas, C. E. (1961). *Loneliness.* Prentice-Hall.

New American Bible, Revised Edition. (2011). Catholic Book Publishing.

Patton, M. Q. (2015). *Qualitative research & evaluation methods: Integrating theory and practice* (4th eds.). SAGE.

Rolfe, G. (2006). Validity, trustworthiness and rigour: Quality and the idea of qualitative research. *Journal of Advanced Nursing, 53*(3), 304–310.

Sandstrom, K. L., Martin, D. D., & Fine, G. A. (2006). *Symbols, selves, and social reality: A symbolic interactionist approach to social psychology and sociology.* Roxbury.

Schmitz, M. (2018, January 10). What does it mean for me to share my faith? *The Catholic Spirit.* https://thecatholicspirit.com/faith/focus-on-faith/ask-father-mike/mean-share-faith/

Seidman, I. E. (2019). *Interviewing as qualitative research: A guide for researchers in educational and social sciences* (5th ed.). Teachers College Press.

Smith, L. T. (2000). Kaupapa Maori research. In M. Battiste (Ed.), *Reclaiming Indigenous voice and vision* (pp. 225–247). University of Columbia Press.

Sultan, N. (2018). *Heuristic inquiry: Researching human experience holistically.* SAGE Publications.

Tran, C. B. A. (2024). *Visit the imprisoned: A heuristic inquiry into the experiences of Catholic detention ministry volunteers* [Doctoral dissertation]. Chapman University Digital Commons. https://doi.org/10.36837/chapman.000531

von Engelhardt, D (2007). The historical and philosophical background of ethics in clinical research. In U. Schmidt, & A. Frewer (Eds.), *History and theory of human experimentation* (pp. 55–70). Franz Steiner Verlag.

Chapter 9 Discussion Questions

1. How does faith sharing as a qualitative research method challenge traditional notions of rigor, trustworthiness, and objectivity in academic research?
2. Tran emphasizes reducing power imbalances between the researcher and collaborators. How does faith sharing foster an egalitarian relationship in the research process, and what are the potential limitations or challenges of achieving true power symmetry in such settings?
3. Reflect on the integration of spirituality into research, as described in the chapter. What ethical and practical considerations should researchers keep in mind when incorporating their faith or spirituality into the methodology, especially in contexts that may involve collaborators?
4. In this study, faith sharing is positioned as a culturally responsive method. How might this approach be adapted to other faith traditions or cultural contexts to authentically honor participants' experiences? What risks exist when attempting to generalize a method beyond its original cultural or religious framework?

TEN

Emancipatory Research Using Critical Feminist Discourse Analysis

Geraldine Mooney Simmie

MY RESEARCH INTEREST AND SPECIALISM are in emancipatory research. This involves scrutinizing how framing social scientific problems in education, in relation to teachers' identities, positionalities, and practices, plays out in contemporary theory, policy, and practice.

My journey as a researcher, striving to establish myself as a social scientific scholar in the expansive field of education, has been both challenging and continuously evolving. It began with a positivistic approach during my doctoral dissertation on the education policy process at Trinity College Dublin (Mooney Simmie, 2009) and has since transitioned to critical and feminist interpretivist studies, which more closely reflect my values, positionality, and identity as a researcher. Currently, I conduct policy research studies that draw from theorizations that crossover between the two traditions of Critical Pedagogy and Feminist Studies. This helps me to search, to research, and to *think with* Freire, hooks, Arendt, and Greene, to name but a few theorists that make meaning for me in relation to re-orienting education from competition and colonization to equality, care, and justice [emancipation].

In order to justify my selection of *Critical Feminist Discourse Analysis* as a research technique in this chapter, I needed to first consider the purpose of education and how it is connected to democracy and the wider world; how contemporary education is framed in mainstream research, policy, and practices; and what levers of power education researchers can call on to radically disrupt this mainstream colonizing discourse.

Contradictory Purposes of Education

The history of education shows that its relationship with schooling evolves and adapts, often shifting in response to crises in the economy and politics (Arendt, 1958/2018). The education policy-making process, at the level of the nation-state, is highly influenced by supranational policy actors (e.g., *Organization for Economic Cooperation and Development* OECD). While the state consults with all vested interests, not all have the same power of influence (e.g., businesses, churches, trade unions, parents/guardians, and civil society) (Althusser, 1971/2014). Today, the needs of the economy and security remain the dominant face of schooling. This policy imperative is increasing exponentially as fast capitalism works to devour democracy, care, and the planet (Edling & Mooney Simmie, 2020; Fraser, 2022).

The philosopher of education, Gert J. Biesta (2020), claimed that education has three interconnected and yet contradictory purposes: (a) the need for qualification is expressed today as lists of attitudes, skills, and knowledge; (b) the need for socialization into the existing culture and status quo; and (c) the need for subjectification, which is concerned with affordances for becoming a subject in one's own right, and at the same time becoming a (responsible) member of society, in associated living with others across multiple communities, such as a citizen of a democratic society (nation state) and more recently a global citizen.

An expansive discourse of education as an emancipatory practice is replete with discursive spaces and gaps for the personal (ethical) project of human becoming as well as the journey of becoming an active, agentic, responsible, and contributing member of society and the wider world. In his book, *The Beautiful Risk of Education*, Biesta (2013) reminds us that education, in words often attributed to the Irish poet W. B. Yeats, is more about "the lighting of a fire rather than the filling of a pail." (p. 1). It is this power of imagination for the primacy of ethics, working within liminal spaces in the gaps between policy and praxis, that gives educators the pedagogical freedom to make a difference in educating for freedom and for securing the critical social consciousness needed for a more just, moral, and caring social, material, cultural, and political world and planet (Freire, 1971/2018; Greene, 1988; hooks, 1994).

Education is, therefore, never innocent or coming from nowhere. Education researchers cannot justifiably proclaim that they are neutral and objective in relation to education, policy, and practices. The educator/researcher is always seeking to turn the gaze of the student in a stated direction (or to study that gaze in a stated direction). This is intentionality, deeply entangled with policy, politics, power, and privilege. Education as a discipline and a moral and political field of practice is underpinned by governing ideologies in relation to what it means today to be human and who, why, and what is decided as overall desired changes.

Today, a neoliberal imaginary shapes education and all public services. Since the mid-1990s, education has opened up from being a social science to becoming more like the natural sciences and applied sciences (Gulbenkian Commission, 1996). The neoliberal imaginary works with primacy to the markets, where other aspects of what it means to be human—moral, social, affective, cultural, and political are positioned as subsidiaries (Tan, 2014). This human capital model increasingly frames education as a data-driven and state-centered system of performance management (Selwyn & Gašević, 2020). This mainstream discourse works as a scientific/entrepreneurial model of hyper-masculinities that manages and measures everything and seeks to reduce all human life to numerical objectification.

Therefore, attempting to identify a research technique that has the power to disrupt this neoliberal imaginary in education and to radically dream otherwise is proving to be immensely challenging and risks being captured, domesticated, and neutralized (Mooney Simmie, 2023a). Today, the field of educational studies appears in many ways to have lost its way as it increasingly moves closer to an atheoretical field without its traditional underpinning of its foundational disciplines and hierarchy of knowers (i.e., social science) and increasingly toward a hierarchy of knowledge (i.e., natural sciences and applied sciences).

Ball (1995) argues that theory serves many purposes in education research studies, especially its capacity to explain, interrupt, disrupt, sap power, and imagine otherwise. For this reason, I assert that all masters' and doctoral theses need a theoretical framework that reveals to the reader the emerging identity and positionality of the education researcher and justifies the selection of the lenses/theoretical perspectives used to examine the (social scientific) problem under interrogation.

Mainstream research and policy in education have today adopted a scientific discourse that is closer to narrow scientism than science, that boasts a normative consensus (predetermined attitudes, skills, and values), and operates as a *Dogmatic Image of Thought* (Deluze, 2004, p. 149) that gives supremacy to abstract thinking reified from the world of experience, from situated knowledge, and from relational ways of being and knowing (Bang, 2017).

Selection of Research Paradigm and Strategy

The two traditions of Critical Pedagogy and Feminist Studies taken together become the research paradigm (overarching umbrella) for my research technique and have something powerful to offer, separately and especially woven together, in terms of disrupting the mainstream neoliberal imaginary in education policy, research, and colonizing practices today.

The field of Critical Pedagogy, arising from the theorizations of Paulo Freire and others in the last fifty years, has convincingly revealed that education is never neutral, that it is a political field of human change in a stated direction that works to reproduce the status quo, to socialize people to know their place in an elite world of hierarchy, power, and privilege (Freire, 1971/2018). Neoliberalism has no interest in forging egalitarian and democratic relations and instead relies on monologic 'banking' models of transmission and elite hierarchies with an over-focus on metrics. This explains why critical pedagogues take the side of the oppressed.

Many reforms today, when closely examined, are framed in the interest of the individual, the institution, and markets (neoliberal framing) and not for the greater good of society or public interest values. Democracy is considered within a 'thin' worldview that seeks civic engagement for compliance within the police state rather than as a dynamic entity that needs to be reborn regularly in the direction of equality, care, and justice in the wider world and planet (Edling & Mooney Simmie, 2020; Mooney Simmie & Edling, 2019).

The field of Feminist Studies, including theorizations of Maxine Greene, Kathleen Lynch, Nancy Fraser, and Donna Haraway, among others, assert that education is primarily a relational process rather than a predominantly product (positivistic) system of *what works*. Relationships rely on pedagogies of recognition and care, authentic dialogue, and the forging of ethical values of trust and solidarity, all of which are upstream of instrumental discourses of *excellence* and *best practices* (Fraser, 2009, 2022; Haraway, 2016; hooks, 1994; Lynch, 2022). Feminist studies put issues of gender to the forefront, and similar to critical pedagogy, which positions social class at the forefront, both recognize the complex ways class, gender, race, ethnicity, and disability intersect. Feminist studies eschew the Cartesian dualism of logical positivism that reduces what it means to be a whole person to positioning in a hierarchical/caste system with strict divisions of labor (see Lynch & Crean, 2019).

Feminist theorizations assert that education invites us to live with paradoxes and to *stay with the trouble* (Haraway, 2016). Feminists aim to complexify rather than reduce the problem. The aim of the current third wave of feminism is to interrogate the framing of policies today to foreground care and intersectionality and reveal what may be missing, forgotten, or otherwise silenced (Mac Lure, 2003).

How Critical Feminist Discourse Analysis Is Used in My Research

The research technique I introduce here is *Critical Feminist Discourse Analysis*. This technique relies on *thinking with* critical and feminist scholars (noted earlier) and working within a worldview (research paradigm) of emancipatory education. It is a disruptive qualitative method because it is theory-rich and can, therefore, disrupt the framing of mainstream discourses in policy, research, and practice. It understands education as a relational and ethical process that needs to provide results but cannot have an output as its primary purpose.

Education needs to be problem-posing and to facilitate (appropriate) risk rather than act as a problem-solving and risk-averse discourse that is predetermined in advance (Mooney Simmie & Moles, 2020). If this *beautiful risk* of education is bypassed, then there is a real danger that we remove education entirely and allow the discourse to be reduced to a limiting discourse of *training* and *disciplining* (Biesta, 2013).

Critical Feminist Discourse Analysis views education from the point of view of the personal and the political, the need for education to proactively support students to overcome their *limit situations* (Freire, 1971/2018), to foreground intersectionality and to include a rich interplay of knowledge with different ways of knowing rather than submit to the supremacy of a *Dogmatic Image of Thought* (Bang, 2017), or a consensus view of values with no requirement for reflexive meaning making outside of the abstract.

I used *Critical Feminist Discourse Analysis* to conduct a critical and feminist scrutiny of the framing of policy documents in relation to the gendered construction of teacher education in Ireland and internationally (Mooney Simmie, 2023 b, c). I examined not only the wording in relation to gender in the documents, what the language and syntax might reveal but also what was missing from the policy texts. I wanted to examine the gendered-construction of policy texts in teacher education. It was at a time in Ireland when gender had become a topic worthy of mention in education policy when there was policy talk about increasing the number of women and girls in STEM education and a policy promise of Equality, Diversity, *and Inclusion* (EDI). It was also at a time when there was increasing evidence of a neoliberal capture of education in Ireland and elsewhere in relation to a hegemony of hyper-masculinities calling for evidence of *what works*—a discourse that was especially subservient to supranational policy experts, such as the OECD (see Mooney Simmie, 2021, 2021b, 2023d).

Key questions that helped my discursive research to reveal the hidden assumptions beneath the framing of this policy problem included the following: How is the problem of gender framed and defined in the policy? What is included, and what appears to be excluded? Who benefits from this framing? Who falls behind and appears to be left out? What is becoming normalized, and how do power and privilege play out in this policy framing? My findings clearly showed that policymakers were defining *gender* in the teacher education documents in *gender neutral* ways. This framing avoided the complex issues involved in a rich definition of gender, including identifying the insidious ways that sexism continues to play out in the gendered construction of teacher education and the power and privilege underpinning the often assumed gendered divisions of labor in the affective system of care so relevant to teacher education and to schooling.

Disrupting Systems of Oppression and Empowering Participants

Critical Feminist Discourse Analysis works as a research technique to disrupt mainstream systems of oppression because it is theory rich and offers the language, ideas, and concepts to scrutinize social scientific problems, to explain otherwise, and to theorize alternatives, especially as it is underpinned by an expansive worldview of education as an emancipatory practice of freedom (Freire, 1971/2018; hooks, 1994; Lazar, 2007; Mac Lure, 2003).

Critical Feminist Discourse Analysis offers the researcher a critical, social, and heuristic device to conduct an affirmative critique of education, a discipline, and a field that disappoints today because of its preoccupation with predetermined outcomes and provided values. I want to leave the reader in no doubt that what is needed is a radical disruption of the neoliberal imaginary.

Otherwise, practitioners are open to exploitation when expected to act as caregivers in a system with an overriding focus on 'the terrors of performativity' (Ball, 2003).

Masters' and doctoral theses that result from using *Critical Feminist Discourse Analysis* will, therefore, need to include some additional chapters that are not found in post-positivistic theses. For example, the researcher will have a chapter telling the reader about their selection and justification of a theoretical framework as an explicit conceptual lens for their study. This will interplay the reflexive positioning of the education researcher with their theoretical (epistemological and ontological) lenses in order to examine their selected problem, i.e., philosophical positioning in relation to the nature of knowledge and the nature of ethical values (Mooney Simmie, 2021a, 2022). The researcher will need to keep a reflexive diary and use vignettes from that in their thesis to inform the reader about their evolving positioning and how their identity changes throughout (Pillow, 2003).

The researcher may also include a chapter dedicated to interrogating the relevant national and international policies that are shaping their topic of study. This policy analysis will reveal how the neoliberal imaginary is playing out in policies today and how this influences the policy framing of their topic. By theorizing and advocating for an alternative framework, the researcher can present a vision for transformative possibilities, offering a path for change within qualitative studies.

Foundational Texts and Important Theorists

Foundational texts from the critical and feminist scholars mentioned earlier help me to understand my epistemological and ontological positioning as a social science researcher and show me why I am invested in taking the side of those who are marginalized by the contemporary oppressive system of schooling. They show how to conduct rigorous research with data trustworthiness and validity while advocating for alternatives to the current neoliberal imaginary for transformative possibility and hope.

I found texts by John Creswell particularly useful for understanding my researcher positioning and for the selection of a research strategy that was imbued with advocacy for emancipation (Creswell & Creswell, 2018). I can recommend a text by Maggie Mac Lure in relation to how to engage with

Discourse Analysis, especially with feminist discourse analysis (Mac Lure, 2003). A book by Michelle Lazar became my prime text (Lazar, 2007), introducing me to the technique of Critical Feminist Discourse Analysis, which I used in published research studies (Mooney Simmie, 2023 b, c). More recently, I brought this collection of texts together to provide better support to early career researchers in a study entitled *Making the Case for Critical Feminist Discourse Analysis of Policy: Decolonizing Educational Research for Critical, Social and Heuristic Purposes*, published online by Sage (Mooney Simmie, 2024).

Critical and feminist studies woven together is a relatively recent field of educational studies—a new field of educational studies that seeks to blur the boundaries between the two traditions of Critical Pedagogy and Feminist Studies in order to re-orient the field of education from the contemporary neoliberal preoccupation with an over-focus on a product model of competition. This over-focus on a product model can be found wherever education is described as management, measurement, and as an exercise in the scientific planning of learning outcomes. Instead, critical and feminist studies allow an opportunity for a more productive dialogue between the traditions that present education as relational and seek to re-orient education in the direction of equality, care, and justice for humans, non-humans, the environment, and the planet. This answers a recent call from UNESCO (2021), seeking a new social contract for education, a new way of repairing injustices from the past, and finding new approaches to the collective consciousness needed for the greater good of society and the green transition for climate justice and sustainability.

Suggestions for Further Reading and References

Althusser, L. (1971/2014). *On the reproduction of capitalism ideology and ideological state apparatuses*. Verso Publishers.

Arendt, H. (1954/2018). The crisis in education. In H. Arendt (Ed.). *Between past and future: Eight exercises in political thought* (pp. 170–193). Penguin.

Ball, S. J. (1995). Intellectuals or technicians? The urgent role of theory in educational studies. *British Journal of Educational Studies, 43*(3), 255–271. http://doi.org/10.1080/00071005.1995.9974036

Ball, S. J. (2003). The teacher's soul and the terrors of performativity. *Journal of Education Policy, 18*(2), 215–228. http://doi.org/10.1080/0268093022000043065

Bang, L. (2017). In the maw of the Ouroboros: An analysis of scientific literacy and democracy. *Cultural Studies of Science Education, 13*(3), 807–822.

Biesta, G. J. J. (2013). *The beautiful risk of education*. Routledge.

Biesta, G. J. J. (2020). Risking ourselves in education: Qualification, socialization, and subjectification revisited. *Educational Theory, 70*(1), 89–104.

Creswell, J. W., & Creswell, J. D. (2018). *Research design qualitative, quantitative, and mixed methods approaches* (5th ed.). Sage Publications.

Deleuze, G. (1968/2004). *Difference and repetition* (P. Patton, Trans.). Columbia University Press.

Edling, S., & Mooney Simmie, G. (2020). *Democracy and teacher education: Dilemmas, challenges and possibilities*. Routledge.

Fraser, N. (2009). *Scales of justice reimagining political space in a globalising world*. Columbia University Press.

Fraser, N. (2022). *Cannibal capitalism. How our system is devouring democracy, care, and the planet—and what we can do about it*. Verso.

Freire, P. (1971/2018). *Pedagogy of the oppressed with a new introduction by Donaldo Macedo and an afterword by Ira Shor*. Bloomsbury.

Greene, M. (1988). *The dialectic of freedom*. Teachers College, Columbia University Press.

Gulbenkian Commission. (1996). *Open the social sciences: Report of the Gulbenkian commission on the restructuring of the social sciences*. Stanford University Press.

Haraway, D. J. (2016). *Staying with the trouble*. Duke University Press.

hooks, b. (1994). *Teaching to transgress: Education as the practice of freedom*. Routledge.

Lazar, M. M.(2007). Feminist critical discourse analysis: Articulating a feminist discourse praxis. *Critical Discourse Studies, 4*(2), 141–164.

Lynch, K. (2022). *Care and capitalism: Why affective equality matters for social justice*. Polity Press.

Lynch, K., & Crean, M. (2019). On the question of cheap things: Regarding a history of the world in seven cheap things by Raj Patel and Jason W. Moore. *Irish Journal of Sociology, 27*(2), 200–207. http://doi.org/10.1177/0791603519835432

Mac Lure, M. (2003). *Discourse in education and social research*. Open University Press.

Mooney Simmie, G. (2009). *The policy implementation process in the upper secondary education system (senior cycle) and videregående skolen in science and mathematics in the Republic of Ireland and the Kingdom of Norway from 1960–2005*. [PhD thesis]. Dublin: Trinity College Dublin. http://www.tara.tcd.ie/handle/2262/90412

Mooney Simmie, G. (2021a). Remaining a student of teaching forever: Critical reflexive insights from a lifetime of multiple teacher identities in the Republic of Ireland. In S. Edling & S. Macrine, (eds). *Professional learning and identities in teaching international narratives of successful teachers*. (pp. 20–35). Routledge: Research in Teacher Education Series.

Mooney Simmie, G. (2021b). Pied Piper of neo liberalism continues to call the tune in the Republic of Ireland: A critical scrutiny of education policy text from 2012 to 2021. *Journal for Critical Education Policy Studies, JCEPS, 19*(2), 427–451.

Mooney Simmie, G. (2022). Suppression of teacher's voices: Agency and freedom within neoliberal masculinist *performativity*. In S. Edling & S. Macrine, (eds). *Transnational feminist politics, education and social justice: Post democracy and post truth*. (pp. 141–154). Bloomsbury Academic.

Mooney Simmie, G. (2023a). Radically dreaming, emancipatory teaching: Supporting teachers as problem-posing intellectuals and activists for a just global world. In T. M. Kress, R. Lake, & E. Stein (eds). *Radically Dreaming: Illuminating Freirean praxis in turbulent times.* (pp. 155–164). DIO Press.

Mooney Simmie, G. (2023b). The gendered construction of teachers' identities and practices: Feminist critical discourse analysis of policy texts in Ireland. *Gender and Education, 35*(3), 282–298.

Mooney Simmie, G. (2023c). The fast globalizing gendered construction of teacher education: A critical feminist research policy analysis of the contemporary reform movement. *Frontiers in Education*, (Vol. 8, Article no. 1113011). Frontiers Media SA. http://doi.org/10.3389/feduc.2023.1113011

Mooney Simmie, G. (2023d). Teacher professional learning: A holistic and cultural endeavour imbued with transformative possibility. *Educational Review, 75*(5), 916–931. https://doi.org/10.1080/00131911.2021.1978398

Mooney Simmie, G. (2024). Making the case for critical feminist discourse analysis of policy: Decolonizing educational research for critical, social and heuristic purposes. In *Sage Research Methods: Diversifying and Decolonizing Research*, (pp. 1–27). Sage Publications Inc. https://doi.org/10.4135/9781529684650

Mooney Simmie, G., & Edling, S. (2019). Teachers' democratic assignment: A critical discourse analysis of teacher education policies in Ireland and Sweden. *Discourse: Studies in the Cultural Politics of Education, 40*(6), 832–846. http://doi.org/10.1080/01596306.2018.1449733

Mooney Simmie, G., & Moles, J. (2020). Teachers' changing subjectivities: Putting the soul to work for the principle of the market or for facilitating risk? *Studies in Philosophy and Education, 39*(4), 383–398. https://link.springer.com/content/pdf/10.1007%2Fs11217-019-09686-9.pdf

Pillow, W. (2003). Confession, catharsis, or cure? Rethinking the uses of reflexivity as methodological power in qualitative research. *International Journal of Qualitative Studies in Education, 16*(2), 175–196. http://doi.org/10.1080/0951839032000060635

Selwyn, N., & Gašević, D. (2020). The datafication of higher education: Discussing the promises and problems. *Teaching in Higher Education, 25*(4), 527–540.

Tan, E. (2014). Human capital theory: A holistic criticism. *Review of Educational Research, 84*(3), 441–445. doi: 10.3102/0034654314532696

UNESCO. (2021). *Reimagining our futures together: A new social contract for education. Report from the International Commission on the Futures of Education.* UNESCO.org. https://www.unesco.org/en/articles/reimagining-our-futures-together-new-social-contract-education.

Chapter 10 Discussion Questions

1. How does Mooney Simmie's journey from positivist to critical and feminist interpretivist paradigms in this chapter reflect the importance of aligning one's research methodology with personal values, positionality, and identity? Discuss the implications of this alignment for educational research.
2. Biesta (2020) identified three purposes of education—qualification, socialization, and subjectification. How do these purposes manifest within contemporary neoliberal education policies, and how might they conflict with the goals of emancipatory education as described in the chapter?
3. In what ways does Critical Feminist Discourse Analysis disrupt the neoliberal imaginary and reframe educational research? Reflect on its potential to reveal hidden assumptions in policy texts and its role in promoting relational and ethical approaches to education.
4. In this chapter, Mooney Simmie highlights the limitations of gender-neutral policy language in addressing sexism and privilege in teacher education. How can education researchers use feminist frameworks to uncover and address gaps in policy, and what challenges might they face in advocating for more inclusive and intersectional approaches?

ELEVEN

Decolonizing Education Research: *Pláticas* as Sites of Reciprocity, Vulnerability, and Reflexivity

Miryam Espinosa-Dulanto

Pláticas in Latino Communities

PLÁTICAS, OFTEN USED WITHIN LATINO communities, serve as a bridge between private experiences and the public sphere. These conversations depict diverse voices and thoughts, weaving together personal memories and collective experiences. Through *pláticas*, Latinos/as/es share individual struggles, joys, and dreams, creating a tapestry of shared understandings. In education research, *pláticas* highlight and connect personal stories that resonate with both local and wider social occurrences, fostering a sense of community and mutual support. Additionally, pláticas symbolize a connection with different worldviews, inviting and recognizing local knowledge and participation.

Invitation to Listen

listen my friend
for we have a thousand-thousand stories to tell
stories to amaze,
stories to horrify.
stories that explain what true community is
and how it is built
and how it is destroyed
stories about place
and home
and devastation
and rebuilding
and characters

and hatred
and kindness
and food
and hunger,
of drink and addiction
of riches and desolation
come sit and listen
to our triumphs
and fears
and share your fears too
for it is through this that we can become friends
and let you leave a shadow of you here with us
and send you home with the phantoms of our collective memory
(Espinosa-Dulanto in Viren, et al., 2024)

Personal Identity and Multiplicity

As a foreign-born, foreign-raised, naturalized USA citizen, I am always identifiable and possibly targeted, discriminated against, exoticized, or used as a token to meet diversity goals as a Hispanic/Latina female. However, official demographic labels do not address the multiplicity of my identity. I am also a Mestiza from the Americas' South, a mother, a grandmother, a community servant, a grassroots organizer, an ethnographer, a teacher educator, and an educational researcher. The multiplicity and diversity of these roles have helped me with my interdisciplinary work, incorporating decolonial Indigenous feminist research methodologies within curriculum theory, critical pedagogies, curriculum development, and education policies for linguistic, racialized, genderized, and culturally minoritized groups.

Reciprocity, Vulnerability, and Reflexivity in *Pláticas*

My research and teaching focus on decolonizing (humanizing) efforts through various scholarly projects that challenge the separation between academic and community engagement. This approach drives my involvement in community work and informs my use of *pláticas* as a research methodology. Fierros and Delgado Bernal (2016) describe *pláticas* as part of the Chicana/Latina feminist methodology that "extends particular ways of knowing" (p. 102) to include other theoretical frameworks that center minoritized individuals' experiences, reflecting and addressing multiple ways in which systems are designed to maintain their oppression. Saavedra & Salazar Perez (2017) suggest using Critical Qualitative Inquiry (CQI) to "reinvent, reimagine research tools that allow a space for reconnection and foster interdependence instead of usurping knowledge and information from our participants . . ." (p. 457), striving for the vulnerability of sharing intimate reflections and discussing our lives during *pláticas*. Fierros and Delgado Bernal (2016) stress that "the space we create with Pláticas requires us to be open to sharing our own stories and be vulnerable as we ask of contributors . . ." (p. 115), with varied topics based on concerns, location, emotions, trust, and respect among those involved, using the language of the group's choice. By using *pláticas*, we can construct knowledge, prioritize everyday experiences, provide a space for healing, and rely on reciprocity, vulnerability, and reflexivity (Flores Carmona et al., 2021).

Navigating Contradictions and Empowering Research

The *pláticas* methodology has a profound impact on research within higher education, particularly in challenging and disrupting systems of oppression. By incorporating the voices and experiences of minoritized groups, this approach empowers research participants and highlights broader systemic and epistemological failures rather than viewing contradictions as individual problems. This methodology fosters a more inclusive and equitable research environment, allowing for a deeper understanding of diverse perspectives and experiences. These efforts are definitely not new. They emerged as responses to mainstream heteropatriarchal experiences that minoritized women had to endure. Early work from Cherríe Moraga and Gloria Anzaldúa (1981), The Latina Feminist Group (2001), and Gloria Anzaldúa (2012) centered unheard, daily life stories as part of their research. More specifically, Dolores Delgado Bernal (2008) recognized 'cultural intuition' as inherited knowledge.

Through *pláticas*, researchers can create meaningful change by addressing and dismantling oppressive structures within academic institutions. By placing minoritized groups at the center of the construction of knowledge, the traditional male-centric higher education curriculum is displaced. In *pláticas*, research participants are recognized as knowledge creators, not only as receivers.

Pláticas are not limited to conducting research in specific settings. They are methodologies grounded in decolonial/anticolonial feminist thought and praxis. For example, minoritized researcher Ruth Behar (1995, 1996) exemplifies this impact through her ethnographic work, where she proposed an anthropology that is lived and written in a personal voice. Behar's writing, often seen as contradictory to traditional values and norms of anthropology and larger institutional practices, underscores the need for methodologies like *pláticas*. Using this approach creates a blatant rupture at the individual level, highlighting a view of the contradictions as part of broader systemic issues.

Furthermore, Calderon Berumen and Espinosa-Dulanto (2020) curated 16 beautiful examples of research done with *pláticas* and *testimonios*. The diversity in this special issue shows the magnificence of centering research outside the traditional male-centric, English-only oppressive structures of USA academic institutions. One article by Manal Hamzeh and colleagues (2020) shares how they draw from "interconnected Arabic and Spanish speaking practices of *haki/pláticas* and *testimonios/shahadat* as acts of linguistic and epistemic disobedience in academia" (p. 251). However, they move deeper to explore decolonization transnationally and linguistically across colonial nation-state borders, racial categories, identities, and art forms.

In another piece, *The poetics aesthetics of testimonios. Subverting "I" for social "I/We." Una lengua que desquicia la academia*, the format, tone, and language usage are acts of rebellion, an act of academic defiance where poetic performance narratives, gathered through *pláticas*, are used to center the story into the memory, the world of un/documented immigrants, with the hopes to present a glimpse of it (Calderon Berumen & Espinosa-Dulanto, 2020).

a foreigner in the land of the powerful
with language and observation skills
is a resource to understand those, the different, the needy
the ones with no-english, foreign parents, new to the land
with a quiet, timid gaze
    sits in the back of the classroom
    to observe the efforts and the failures
    the non-communication attempts
want to help you, do it my way, in english of course
i'm doing my best, following what i understood, in mixteco and castellano

got no answers
    instead brought a million questions
        un/felt pain
        un/lived anger
        un/certainty, doubt, awareness . . .
having privilege to quietly observe, record, reflect
    the ables and dis/ables in others
ethnographically learning
    deploying understanding, support, and mentoring
while advancing "my research," my academic endeavor
    strange things happened in the land of the free
    the same reasons one is deeply discriminated
got me the research assistant job
got me into my doctoral program
on time, got me, stamped and ready
    to become legal in the U.S. academe
got me to the realization
    had I crossed to the other side?

the life i left behind
el no poder, el no haber hecho, el haber abandonado, el huir
to *Anzaldúa's herida abierta*, another border, a land divider
to embrace the path of decolonizing
to the testimonio today (Espinosa-Dulanto, 2020)

Grounding *pláticas* methodologies in decolonial/anticolonial Chicana/Latina feminist thought, I concur with Sofia Villenas' (1996) reflection on *contradictory identities* as a fluid space where collusion, oppositionality, complicity, and subversion flourish. For Villenas, as for many of us in USA academia, *pláticas* enable us to be in both worlds and respectfully disseminate the knowledge of our communities.

How to Implement *Pláticas* in Educational Research

In the type of research I am engaged in, *pláticas* are an essential part of the process of gathering information while (a) honoring both researchers' and research participants' epistemological positions, (b) centering on minoritized individuals' experiences, (c) grounding participants as holders and creators of knowledge, (d) becoming potential spaces for healing, and (e) collectively reciprocating to include being vulnerable, reflective, and open to the unexpected.

Despite the mainstream expectation that success can be achieved through step-by-step methods, *pláticas* are inherently demanding and require a balance of structure and flexibility. Their complexity, richness, and depth make it futile to apply linear processes, as they cannot be fully captured by a prescribed methodology.

This raises some questions for researchers: How do I "participate" and/or "host" a *plática* for my research? Even though I identified and numbered key areas, I still find it unachievable to support the idea of a step-by-step method for *pláticas*. To clarify the process, I invite you, the reader, to join me in a *plática*. In this section, I aim to show how a *plática* can be built within the research space and how researchers and participants can create a sense of community and belonging, which is essential for the *plática* to succeed. Let's explore this by considering several areas: time, community and individual experiences, life events, healing space, research goals, and reflective learning.

Time or Community?

As soon as I wrote the invitation, I realized that I couldn't define which step or area I needed to tackle first.

I smiled . . . as I realized—again—that research goals are important too . . . as they guide our research path and allow us to assess it . . . but then, we would be back in an extractive, mainstream, colonizing mindset. Let's focus, try to move on, and begin with time. In my experience, *time* is probably one of the most challenging aspects of building the *pláticas*' space when working in a traditional institution organized around a schedule, with deadlines to produce, assess, report, and learn.

For example, there is a deadline to submit this manuscript, yet my heart is broken. I just lost my younger brother. I want to mourn; I want to remember; I want to cry; I want . . . yet here I am in front of a computer screen typing these words . . . or fulfilling my work duties, standing in front of a class teaching about diversity, equity, and inclusion. . . . All good, yet the vulnerable side of the instructor must be set aside to benefit a schedule, all to fulfill the mission and vision of the institution for which I work. There is no invitation to the cacophony of the world, the vibrancy of the borderlands, or the political debates—only carefully curated stories that may help achieve the institution's strategic planning. *Pláticas* have that challenge at their core, as the invitation is to embrace and host the creation of a collective yet deeply personal space where there is *time* to reflect and share so I/we may be embraced by others who have experienced grief themselves.

With a 60–80-hour work week that feels like 1,000, I have neither the time nor the permission to engage in these reflections. In a *pláticas* setting, I would have shared and invited others to share their traditions of mourning or simply provided a space to voice the tormenting questions that consume me.

How do you remember?
How do you separate yourself from the dead?
How do you live without the part of you that is no longer alive?

Writing this piece in solitude makes me miss the community in *pláticas* even more. . . . It is just a monological world of pain that keeps on wondering . . . then stops to breathe . . . starts again . . . goes on with the daily routine—work . . . home. All around, a silent, overpowering numbness pressures my chest and chokes me . . . ops . . . I'm not alone; I'm surrounded by empty smiles, productive people reminding me about timetables, deadlines, and assessments. . . . As a well-trained minoritized individual, my levels of resilience should be resourceful now. Yet, as much as my whole being rebels, my questions are shut down entirely, and it is time for a full automatic pilot.

Usually, in *pláticas*, the group begins with an agreement to focus the conversation on the content that the researcher and members are working on, but it is also understood that the space is flexible enough to accommodate the participants' needs. It is important to state that every group of *pláticas* I have experienced schedules meetings (weekly, biweekly, or monthly) with a specific start time but no set end time—usually in the evenings—in a setting outside the workspace that is suitable for a long meeting, typically 3–4 hours. We also plan ahead with readings or writing that will be discussed in relation to the topic—members are seriously prepared to actively engage. However, all this is flexible enough to include celebrations, cathartic moments, cries, current events, domestic distractions, nice dinners—whatever we may need as individuals to maintain our well-being and productivity.

In summary, we prioritize serious work and engagement while also embracing the inclusion of individual happenings. Our work is intertwined with our humanity, and reciprocity, vulnerability, and reflexivity are intrinsically shared. We say YES to serious work and engagement, and NO to silence or isolation. Thus, step one mutates into steps two, three, four, and five in a process so organic, dynamic, and fluid that there is no longer a separation. In *pláticas*, we are building a community of trust and care, honoring researchers' and participants' epistemological positions while centering and learning from individual and collective experiences. All of these elements are woven into fluid, respectful, and heartfelt conversations that immerse and smoothly move the process to include spaces for healing and collective reciprocity, including being vulnerable, reflective, and open to accepting diversity, deepening our collective journey with the help of the *pláticas*.

Going back to the current moment, to the overwhelming silence in my office, the overpowering feeling of loss, the loudness of the questions filling my heart in contrast to the barrenness of answers and lack of support . . . needing my community, I found a memory and remembered my friend Maria with a suggestion:

say his name
we will remember together
say his name . . .
so here it is dear brother,
RAFAEL VICENTE ESPINOSA DULANTO, *presente*
you are remembered, you are with me, you are *presente*

In my experience, the success of *pláticas* hinges on the principles of reciprocity, vulnerability, and reflexivity. By respecting the epistemological positions of both researchers and participants, focusing on the experiences of minoritized individuals, and acknowledging participants as both holders and creators of knowledge, *pláticas* can become spaces for healing. These discussions blend fluid, respectful, and heartfelt exchanges, guiding the process forward smoothly and creating a collective journey enriched by the shared wisdom and experiences of everyone involved.

Suggestions for Further Reading

Alvarez, S., Martínez, J. L., Salamanca, A., Salamanca, E., & Reyna, R., (2021). Cosecha voices: Migrant farmworker students, pedagogy, voice, and self-determination. *Harvard Educational Review, 91*(3), 319–340.

Barrios de Chúngara, D. & Viezzer, M. (1978). Let me speak! Testimony of a woman in the Bolivian mines (Trans. V. Ortiz). Monthly Review Press.

Cruz, C. (2001). Toward an epistemology of a Brown body. *International Journal of Qualitative Studies in Education, 14*(5), 657–669.

Delgado Bernal, D. (1998). Using Chicana feminist epistemology in educational research. *Harvard Educational Review, 68*(4), 555–582.

Delgado Bernal, D., Flores, A. I., Gaxiola Serrano, T. J., & Morales, S. (2023). An introduction: Chicana/Latina feminista pláticas in educational research. *International Journal of Qualitative Studies in Education, 36*(9), 1627–1630.

Elenes, A.C. (2000). Chicana feminist narratives and the politics of the self. *Frontiers: A Journal of Women Studies, 21*(3), 105–123.

González, F. E. (1998). *The formations of Mexicanness: Trenzas de identidades multiples: The development of womanhood among young Mexicanas: Braids of multiple identities.* [Doctoral dissertation]. University of California, Davis.

Menchú, R., & Burgos, E. (1985). *Me llamo Rigoberta Menchú y así me nació la consciencia.* México, DF: Siglo XXI Ed.

Morales, S., Flores, A. I., Gaxiola Serrano, T. J., & Delgado Bernal, D. (2023). Feminista pláticas as a methodological disruption: drawing upon embodied knowledge, vulnerability, healing, and resistance. *International Journal of Qualitative Studies in Education, 36*(9), 1631–1643.

Perez, E. (1999). *The decolonial imaginary: Writing Chicanas into history.* Indiana University Press.

Rodríguez, C. O. (2018). The # shitholes Syllabus. *The Radical Teacher*, (111), 30–34.

References

Anzaldúa, G. (2012). *Borderlands / La Frontera: The new Mestiza (4th ed).* Aunt Lute Books.

Behar, R. (1995). Writing in my father's name: A diary of translated woman's first year. In Behar, R. & Gordon, D. (Eds.), *Women Writing Culture.* University of California Press (pp. 65-84).

Behar, R. (1996). *The vulnerable observer: Anthropology that breaks your heart.* Beacon Press.

Calderon Berumen, F. & Espinosa-Dulanto, M. (2020). Enlazando/rompiendo fronteras in Curriculum theory: Testimonio research's aesthetic dimensions. *Journal of Curriculum & Pedagogy, 17*(3), 233–330.

Delgado Bernal, D., Aleman, E., & Flores Carmona, J. (2008). Transnational and transgenerational Latina/o cultural citizenship among kindergarteners, their parents, and university students in Utah. *Social Justice 35*(1), 28–49.

Delgado Bernal, D. & Villalpando, O. (2002). An apartheid of knowledge in academia: The struggle over the "legitimate" knowledge of faculty of color. *Equity & Excellence in Education, 35*(2),169–180.

Espinosa-Dulanto, M. & Calderon-Berumen, F. (2020). The poetics aesthetics of testimonios. Subverting "I" for social "I/We." Una lengua que desquicia la academia. *Journal of Curriculum and Pedagogy, 17*(3): 242–246. https://doi.org/10.1080/15505170.2020.1837694

Fierros, C. & Delgado Bernal, D. (2016). Vamos a platicar: The contours of pláticas as Chicana/Latina feminist methodology. *Chicana/Latina Studies 15*(2), 98–121.

Flores Carmona, J., Hamzeh, M., Delgado Bernal, D., & Hassan Zareer, I. (2021). Theorizing knowledge with pláticas: Moving toward transformative qualitative inquiries. *Qualitative Inquiry, 27*(10), 1213–1220.

Hamzeh, M., Carmona, J. F., Sánchez, M. E. H., Bernal, D. D., & Bejarano, C. (2020). Haki/pláticas~testimonios/shahadat: Arabyya feminista decolonial praxis. *Journal of Curriculum and Pedagogy, 17*(3), 250–265.

Latina Feminist Group. (2002). *Telling to live: Latina feminist testimonios* (Latin America Otherwise). Duke University Press.

Moraga, C. & Anzaldua, G. (1981). *This bridge called my back: Writings by radical women of color.* Persephone Press.

Saavedra, C. & Salazar Perez, M. (2017). Chicana/Latina feminist critical qualitative inquiry. Meditations on global solidarity, spirituality, and the land. *International Review of Qualitative Research. 10*(4), 450–467.

Villenas, S. (1996). The colonizer/colonized Chicana ethnographer: Identity, marginalization, and co-optation in the field. *Harvard Educational Review, 66*(4), 711–731.

Villenas, S. (2005). Latina literacies in convivencia: Communal spaces of teaching and learning. *Anthropology & Education Quarterly 36*(3), 273–77.

Viren, V., Espinosa-Dulanto, M., Lewis, K., & Lerma, E. (2024). Repast: A collective autoethnographic process of meaning-making. *Rio Bravo: A Journal of the Borderlands. 25*, 107–115.

Chapter 11 Discussion Questions

1. How does the methodology of *pláticas* challenge traditional research practices in higher education? Discuss how embracing principles such as reciprocity, vulnerability, and reflexivity in *pláticas* might transform both the research process and its outcomes.
2. Reflect on the role of personal identity in shaping the methodology of *pláticas*. How do the experiences and identities of researchers and participants influence the construction of knowledge, and why is this important in education research?
3. How do *pláticas* foster a sense of community and healing among participants? Consider how this methodology bridges personal experiences with collective narratives and analyze its potential impact on addressing systemic inequities.
4. The chapter discusses the tension between academic expectations and the human experiences of researchers and participants. How can the use of *pláticas* help navigate these contradictions, and what are the implications for researchers working within institutional constraints?

TWELVE

Framing Participatory Action Research (PAR) as a Stance

Maranda C. Ward

As a stance to research, participatory action research (PAR) is an epistemological approach to inquiry that counters speaking for others, classifying their identities, and interpreting, in isolation, the meaning of their lives. Given this description of PAR, I designed a qualitative PAR study as my dissertation. PAR dissertations are designed so that "the end result should be that the data analysis is pushed by relevant literature, and the literature should be extended through the contribution of this action research" (Herr & Anderson, 2005, p. 84). There are key steps doctoral students can follow to apply this PAR stance to their own research (Ward, 2020).

PAR is a research stance with historical relevance for a range of research methodologies. Using arts-based research (ABR) methods, my study invited young adults to reflect on the privilege attached to their peer educator identities while enrolled in my community-based education program while educating their so-called *at-risk* peers who shared their disavowed identities as urban youth. I invited these young adults to create an identity map (Futch & Fine, 2014) of what it meant to be a peer educator, and we discussed this in a recorded interview. I poetically transcribed these interviews into data poems. The youth attended research team meetings to confirm their individual poems and coauthor group poems that talked back to the literature that attempted to disparage them (Ward, 2020).

My commitment to honoring youth expertise is reflected in the use of a PAR stance, which disrupts the power imbalance between the researcher and *the researched* by inviting groups marginalized in research to influence how their data is analyzed, interpreted, and represented (Ayala, 2009; Fine, 2009; Torre, 2009). As such, my study expanded existing discourses about these identities by foregrounding youth stories. This approach is especially important for making sense of the prevailing youth identity discourse that suggests the subjective experiences of urban youth and peer educators matter for how they see and act as themselves.

Epistemology

Crotty (1998) suggested that epistemology is an "attempt to explain how we know what we know and to determine the status to be ascribed to the understandings we reach" (p. 18). Of all the paradigmatic turns in social science inquiry, postmodernism is one such epistemology that explains how researchers make sense of what and how we know. St. Pierre (2011) noted that the standards that discipline the collecting, analyzing, and interpreting of qualitative data in research have been so subscribed that "we've forgotten we made it up" (p. 613). Postmodern thought allows researchers to reimagine other ways to do research. Refusing to triangulate, prove reliability and validity, and move towards generalizability is indicative of how postmodernism centers this study's philosophical intent on preserving multiple ways of knowing.

Postmodernism is the epistemology that suitably complements the PAR stance that framed my research design. A PAR stance rooted in postmodernism offered a democratic questioning of who has power, how they get it, and what they do with it. Lincoln, et al. (2011) describe postmodernism as a "transformation based on the democratic participation between the researcher and subject" (p. 114). This democratic participation enabled me to engage youth in a process of co-constructing and interpreting the narratives, beliefs, and representations tied to their own identities. The investigation of how youth negotiate their performed identities as urban youth and as peer educators capitalized on the study's democratic participation to honor youth voices, including multiple meanings and variable self-representations.

A postmodern perspective, and therefore PAR stance, is evident in how my study was designed to facilitate and encourage youth to creatively and actively contribute to the research process. This study was based on the premise that youth come to the research performing their identities. It was also designed for youth to reflect upon their identity performances as storytellers. In this capacity, the youth assumed research roles to construct their narrative identities that reflect on their storytelling ability to be "multiple, partial, unknowable, [and] resignifying of the self" (Kumashiro, 2001, p. 3).

The widely held beliefs about who urban youth are and how they perform a range of identities seldom come directly from the perspectives of urban youth.

This research challenged, disrupted, and retold what was known, understood, and shared about urban youth. In this quest, the research deliberately refused the oversimplification of urban youth. This meant that the research team embraced and questioned any contradictions that emerged to retell and capture how they performed their identities. To this end, the research design also took into consideration that "translation and research practices can result in speaking against oneself as a non-dominant researcher" (Seth, 1981, as cited in Cannella & Lincoln, 2007, p. 321). Ultimately, this study reshaped the discourse on what is assumed about urban youth and peer educators.

A PAR stance does not come without challenges. The first possible challenge to a PAR stance is that there may be a tendency to valorize youth voices without first problematizing them. Within my PAR study, youth voice was celebrated and equally subject to critique. A second possible challenge with this design was that the youth were invited to serve in research capacities that may not be easy to assume. Therefore, providing training was important.

Additionally, a PAR stance must create space for varying levels of participation. I used two research phases that included clearly marked entry and exit paths to allow youth to decide their degrees of participation, an idea modeled after Tuck and colleagues' (2008) PAR study. Further, a PAR stance may presume that the study's youth need a validating space created for them to theorize, reflect, and act on and out their identity performances. The research process should not solely assume credit for what the youth share, produce, and perform. Finally, a PAR stance is based on the premise that the youth will offer new and different narratives to the discourses that represent their identities. Quite the contrary, the youth may express satisfaction with and/or indifference about existing conceptualizations of their identities.

Disrupting Systems of Oppression and Empowering Participants

While acknowledging the challenges, my study capitalized on the strengths of a PAR stance. There is a privileging of multiple stories, identities, and ideas, as well as researcher reflexivity that comes with such privileging. What this means is that there was no need for analytic consensus because various ways of thinking about and representing identities were welcomed. PAR also honors youth as experts and engaged them in collective inquiry as participants of a research team. This research process provided youth with the credit for all the theorizing and knowledge production they often do but may not formally consider. Additionally, my use of arts-based inquiry made my PAR stance to research that much more accessible and engaging.

The process of engaging youth in research roles included their participation in collecting and analyzing data and collaboratively deciding how best to represent and disseminate findings. This collaborative approach to interpretation helped dismantle the "educational elitism" (Cannella & Lincoln, 2007, p. 323) that often limits who is seen as capable of contributing expert knowledge to research. The youth had the ability to co-create data as they engaged in a research process focused on action as a natural extension of their advocacy roles as former peer educators. This two-phase research design organically allowed for autonomous decisions by youth for how they wanted to participate.

It is worth noting how I positioned myself in the research among the peer educators as the lead researcher as well as their former program director and mentor. As the lead researcher, I took responsibility for data analysis and interpretation. I also provided opportunities for the youth to provide input and feedback throughout the writing process to ensure that what was said, understood, and represented honored the process of the PAR stance to this research. I did not offer apologies for my interpretations, as I was an equal member of the research team who questioned, critiqued, and co-created with the youth. The power and authority attached to both of my positions (and identities) affected the process of telling and re-telling their (and my own) experiences and observations. My role and background as the lead researcher in the process remained transparent, including the impetus for the research and prior relationships to the peer educators and fields of peer education and positive youth development (PYD).

As the lead researcher, I brought assumptions, investments, and expectations to my youth identity inquiry. These assumptions, investments, and expectations, in part, stemmed from the fact that I am a former urban youth and former peer educator. I acknowledge and challenge these assumptions and my observed experiences working with and for urban youth and peer educators. As a community educator, by training with a background in PYD, public health, and service learning, I understand the diversity and complexity of urban youth and of peer educators. These assumptions, expectations, and investments are important elements of my subjectivity that I worked through in this study. I wrote at length about the need to memo my thoughts and decisions.

PAR is an emancipatory approach to acknowledging subjectivity. My subjective experiences led me to this inquiry and uniquely positioned me to pursue what Glesne and Peshkin (1992) describe as "backyard research" (p. 22) for several reasons. I maximized the relationships and rapport I established with the youth in my program to encourage them to invest in developing more integrated representations of themselves so that the world can view them accurately. My program integrates the arts, peer education, and PYD, which were all significant features of my research design. Given my unprecedented access to these youth peer educators, the research meaningfully engaged and validated them as authors and sustained momentum beyond the research process. Nonetheless, the same potential strengths of this research may double as limitations due to the power and privileges that come with my multiple situated positions in their lives.

Some researchers may take issue with selecting research participants who were too familiar with the lead researcher. Because of established relationships and rapport, the comfort levels may contribute to straying from the protocols. The youth also knew one another. The youth may have felt pressure to perform in particular ways, knowing that their identities were not anonymous. Because comparisons were made between individual responses and collective responses, there may have been the perception of peer pressure to offer socially acceptable responses. De-identifying the data and welcoming multiple voices for group analysis lessened emotional discomfort, performance anxiety, and other affective risks.

Foundational Texts and Important Theorists

PAR is rooted in the tradition of action research that dates back to the 1940s when Kurt Lewin attempted to bridge the divide between social practice and psychological thought (Fine et al., 2004). A PAR stance can be applied to quantitative, qualitative, or mixed methods designs, but ultimately, "at its core, it articulates a recognition that knowledge is produced in collaboration and in action" (Fine et al., 2004, p. 173). PAR privileges the communities that are typically disengaged in research by centering them in the research process to frame, design, analyze, and act on social justice-oriented research in ways that bring about social change (Ayala, 2009; Fine, 2009; Torre, 2009). My PAR stance was guided by Torre's (2009) seven key assumptions that contribute to effectively applying a PAR stance in research.

- First, anyone can conduct research. This study, which utilized a PAR stance, acknowledged that all youth had the "right to research" (Appadurai, 2006, p. 167). Therefore, I led training in PAR and ABR methods to enhance the youth's comfort in co-creating knowledge.
- Second, there is a fullness of lived experience. I put into conversation what youth said about their identities with what was said about their identities. This explains why I reviewed and analyzed (and re-narrated as co-developed poems) the conceptualizations of their identities during the PAR training and meeting.
- Third, this stance acknowledges the vulnerabilities and risks involved in research. In my study, I made sure to highlight the seemingly disparate *individual* and *group* representations of their identities.
- This idea led to the fourth assumption that this PAR stance also made clear that the research design makes room for shifting identities. The youth wanted to reclaim the meanings of urban youth identity and re-presented this reframing at our public art research exhibit.
- Fifth, the stance is increasingly useful in understanding that youth value some stories over others and, therefore, that comes through in what they see and count in their reflections in the data collection, analysis, interpretation, and outcomes of the research. It was important to honor yet problematize all ideas.
- Sixth, the PAR stance values multiple methods to get at layers of meaning. This step was helpful as I relied on multiple arts-based methods in my research.
- Seventh, the study intentionally elicited varying levels of participation—explaining the two phases I relied on for the research. These included their individual contributions as participants in the research and their group contributions as participants with research roles.

Some PAR researchers and scholars may argue against the PAR merits of a study that does not engage its participants as co-researchers. The tenets of PAR are not contingent on how involved the youth are from the inception to the dissemination of the study but rather with the philosophical intentions behind their participation (Ayala, 2009; Cahill, 2006; Cammarota & Fine,

2008; Ginwright et al., 2005; Guishard et al., 2005; Silva et al., 2002). Case in point, my PAR study allowed the youth to determine their level of participation. Some youth decided to participate only in the interviews.

Some opted to participate only in the PAR and ABR trainings after their interviews. Others continued on to poetically transcribe their interviews, coding the analytic data poems for themes, and helped to display the data in the public art exhibit. Because of the labor intensive nature of this study, the youth were at liberty to engage in the aspects of the study that most interested them. The strength of this tiered participation schema is that it resembles the participation schema of my peer education program and makes room for youth autonomy and agency throughout the research process. The challenge of this approach was the perceived interruption in the continuity of ideas or youth interpretations that may have contributed to uncertain, minimal, or insufficient data in some aspects of the research inquiry.

It is worth noting that Torre's (2009) seven PAR assumptions fueled my study's PAR aims for social change. A PAR stance credits such change as an ongoing expectation rather than merely an outcome of the research. Kim (2012) describes any action research as bringing together "action, reflection, theory, and practice" (p. 1). What this meant for my PAR study was that the *action* became the research, the *reflection* happened through the methods, the conceptual framework provided a *theory-based* lens to understand the data, and the *practice* stemmed from the resulting performed identities in our public arts research exhibit. This research design also reflected my philosophical commitments to validate youth as the experts on their lives and, at the same time, illustrate the messiness of the complex identities they embrace and perform.

Suggestions for Further Reading and References

Appadurai, A. (2006). The right to research. *Globalisation, Societies and Education, 4*(2), 167–177. https://doi.org/10.1080/14767720600750696

Ayala, J. (2009). Split scenes, converging visions: The ethical terrains where PAR and borderlands scholarship meet. *Urban Review, 41*(1), 66–84. http://doi.org/10.1007/s11256-008-0095-9

Cahill, C. (2006). "At risk"? The fed up honeys re-present the gentrification of the lower east side. *Women's Studies Quarterly, 34*(1/2), 334–363.

Cammarota, J. & Fine, M. (Eds.). (2008). *Revolutionizing education: Youth participatory action research in motion*. Routledge.

Cannella, G. & Lincoln, Y. (2007). Predatory vs. dialogic ethics: Constructing an illusion or ethical practice as the core of research methods. *Qualitative Inquiry, 13*(3), 315–335. http://doi.org/10.1177/1077800406297648

Crotty, M. (1998). *The foundations of social research: Meaning and perspective in the research process*. SAGE.

Fine, M. (1994). Working the hyphens: Reinventing self and other in qualitative research. In N. K. Denzin & Y. S. Lincoln (Eds.), *Handbook of Qualitative Research* (pp. 70–82). SAGE.

Fine, M. (2009). Postcards from metro America: Reflections on youth participatory action research for urban justice. *Urban Review, 41*(1), 1–6. http://doi.org/10.1007/s11256-008-0099-5

Fine, M., Torre, M. E., Boudin, K., Bowen, I., Clark, J., & Hylton, D. (2004). *Echoes: Youth documenting and performing the legacy of Brown v. Board of Education*. Teachers College Press.

Futch, V. A., & Fine, M. (2014). Mapping as method: History and theoretical commitments. *Qualitative research in psychology, 11*(1), 42–59. http://doi.org/10.1080/14780887.2012.719070

Ginwright, S. A., Cammarota, J., & Noguera, P. (2005). Youth, social justice, and communities: Toward a theory of urban youth policy. *Social Justice, 32*(3), 24–40.

Glesne, C., & Peshkin. A. (1992). *Becoming qualitative researchers: An introduction*. Longman.

Guishard, M., Fine, M., Doyle, C., Jackson, J., Singleton, S., & Staten, T. (2005). The Bronx on the move: Participatory consultation with mothers and youth. *Journal of Educational and Psychological Consultation, 16*(1–2), 35–54. http://doi.org/10.1080/10474412.2005.9669526

Herr, K. & Anderson, G. L. (2005). *The action research dissertation: A guide for students and faculty*. SAGE.

Kim, J. (2012). Teacher action as *Bildung*: An application of Gadamer's philosophical hermeneutics to teacher professional development. *Journal of Curriculum Studies*, 1–15. http://doi.org/10.1080/00220272.2012.702224

Kumashiro, K. (2001). "Posts" perspectives on anti-oppressive education in social studies, English, mathematics and science classrooms. *Educational Researcher, 30*(3), 3–12.

Lincoln, Y. S., Lynham, S. A., & Guba, E. G. (2011). Paradigmatic controversies, contradiction, and emerging confluences, revisited. In N. K. Denzon & Y. S. Lincoln (Eds.), *Handbook of Qualitative Research* (4th ed.) (pp. 97–128). SAGE.

Silva, E., Zimmerman, K., & Erbstein, N. (2002). *Youth REP step by step: An introduction to youth-led research and evaluation. Youth in Focus*. Kellogg Foundation.

St. Pierre, E. A. (2011). Anything can happen and does. *Cultural Studies-Critical Methodologies, 11*(4), 386–389.

Torre, E. (2009). Participatory action research and critical race theory: Fueling spaces for nosotras to research. *Urban Review, 41*, 106–120. http://doi.org/10.1007/s11256-008-0097-7

Tuck, E. Allen, J., Bacha, M, Morales, A., Quinter, S., Thompson, J., & Tuck, M. (2008). PAR praxes for now and future change: The collective of researchers on educational disappointment and desire. In J. Cammarota & M. Fine (Eds.), *Revolutionizing education: Youth participatory action research in motion* (pp. 49–83). Routledge.

Ward, M.C. (2020). How an arts-based youth participatory action research study can prevent further marginalizing a vulnerable research population. In K. Thoma (Ed.), *SAGE research methods cases*. https://doi.org/10.4135/9781529740110

Chapter 12 Discussion Questions

1. Ward discusses how the postmodern epistemology complements the PAR stance in disrupting power imbalances and privileging multiple ways of knowing. How might other epistemological approaches (e.g., critical theory) align or clash with the PAR methodology used in this study? Provide examples of how these alternative paradigms could influence the design and outcomes of a similar research project.
2. The chapter highlights challenges in celebrating youth voices without problematizing them and managing their roles as research participants. How can researchers balance honoring participant contributions while maintaining a critical stance?
3. Ward emphasizes the importance of addressing ethical considerations in *backyard research*, particularly when studies involve pre-existing relationships and the influence of researcher power dynamics. What ethical considerations should be prioritized in such settings, and how can researchers mitigate risks of undue influence or participant discomfort?
4. Ward's study employed arts-based methods, such as identity mapping and poetic transcription, to capture and represent youth identities. How might arts-based approaches be integrated into your field of study or professional practice to address complex social issues?

THIRTEEN

Collective Narrative: Honoring the Power of Group Dialogue and Storytelling

Nicole Roady

STORYTELLING PROVIDES OPPORTUNITIES FOR PEOPLE to gain clarity and a new perspective on their lived experiences as they engage in reflexive dialogue with others (Latta & Kim, 2011). By centering on stories, collective narrative research embraces the dialectics of being more fully human in a world that challenges individuals' innate curiosity and compassion (Berryman et al., 2013). The focus on collective narratives emphasizes the power of solidarity and community as the research aims to "transition from individual awareness to collective social action, from individual isolation to collective consciousness" (SooHoo, 2006, p. 185). Analyzing the stories of different individuals and their shared challenges can create an understanding of specific social contexts and foster collective agency toward more socially just initiatives (Broadhurst et al., 2021).

Collective and co-constructed narrative inquiry involves intense collaboration with research participants, referred to as co-narrators, co-constructors, or collaborators. In small dialogue groups of four-to-seven people, co-constructors guide the research and direction of the study with content deemed valuable and vital to their lives or professional practice. Aspects of collective or co-constructed narrative research design intend to be culturally responsive to "raise consciousness of colonizing research traditions" (Berryman et al., 2013, p. 13) and seek to understand the perspectives and stories of individuals in challenging political and social contexts. In this chapter, I detail the process for engaging in a *bricolage* (methods constructed from a diverse range of available ideas and experiences) of narrative inquiry methods with an intentional, humanistic, and anti-oppressive framework. Through dialogue sessions, reflexive journaling, and reflective individual conversations, collective and co-constructed narrative inquiry empowers participants to engage deeply and challenge the normative standards of research.

Together in Dialogue: Group Dialogue Sessions

Collective and co-constructed narrative inquiry is a bricolage of qualitative methodologies that I utilized when conducting my doctoral dissertation in educational studies. To gain insight into the co-narrators' lives and collective experiences as teachers, dialogue sessions were held with a group of five teachers, one teacher assistant, and myself at a private, secular independent PK–8th grade school in California (Leavy, 2017; Marshall & Rossman, 2016; Roady, 2024) over an academic school year. In total, the group met twelve times over the 2023–2024 school year. While not every collaborator was able to be present for every dialogue session, there were at least five collaborators present for each session. Each group dialogue session ranged from 50 to 75 minutes. These conversations were co-constructed to reflect the diversity, equity, inclusion, and social justice (DEIJ) content that interested the group members, as "conversations are marked by equality among participants and by the flexibility to allow participants to establish forms and topics appropriate to their group inquiry" (Clandinin & Connelly, 2000, p. 109).

Instead of coming to sessions with predetermined questions, I collaborated with the group about the content and planned sessions that served their passions and interests. This study's core was storytelling and the desire of participants to learn from one another. Just as our experiences as human beings differ, our classroom content and cultures vary significantly across the school site. Collaborating on the content allowed for connections across content, grade level, and expertise. It also served as a method that holistically spoke to people's desire to learn as educators and individuals. It allowed for the sharing of various artifacts, such as articles, books, podcasts, and art (Lewis & Adeney, 2014). As Kim (2016) expressed, "There is much to discover, explore, and search through for meaning in the artifacts that our storytellers might share with us" (p. 178). They contributed to our dialogue sessions through news articles, social media posts, podcasts, and personal anecdotes related to issues of racism, sexism, and classism. Honoring their experiences and sources of learning was an essential aspect of this collaborative narrative inquiry. Through a group text thread, the group kept in contact over breaks and times when we did not convene. This text thread was a source of connection for this collaborative group and represented the developing relationships among the group.

The sessions began with a check-in point for co-narrators to establish comfort and mentally engage in the narrative inquiry space. Because the collaborators on this study were from the same educational community, there was often a cross-over of experiences or some discussion topics that naturally occurred among educators in shared spaces. The first session focused on personal stories and centered on my question regarding each person's catalyst to engage in DEIJ work personally or professionally. Relationships and trust were integral to this collective narrative study (Lewis & Adeney, 2014), so I guided the group through a reflective activity where members created roadmaps to share their personal history and why DEIJ work matters to them.

After the first session, it was evident through individual interviews and group reflections that comfort and openness were established. For the remaining sessions, we alternated between topics of interest from co-constructors and issues occurring on campus with accompanying chapters and articles that I provided to spur dialogue and critical thought. The group engaged in readings by bell hooks (1994; 2003) and Paulo Freire (1985; 2005; 2018; 2021a; 2021b) and various news articles about political and social issues in the United States. Using the articles, media, or any other referenced material as a jumping-off point, the co-narrator or I, who derived the session's topic, started the group discussion with a question or comment regarding the content. This initial question often started the flow of conversation, and from there, the aim was to allow the educators' stories to take center stage. I often contributed as both a thought partner and active listener to balance my role as a researcher and co-collaborator.

As Clandinin and Connelly (2000) explained, "Conversation entails listening. The listener's response may constitute a probe into experience that takes the representation of experience far beyond what is possible in an interview" (p. 109). These deep connections are fostered by probing to learn more about one another and made possible through establishing trust and consideration for those in dialogue with one another (Clandinin & Connelly, 2000). Conversations often flowed in many different directions, so my data reflected the perspectives and unique experiences of the co-constructors. Given my focus on the lived experiences and meaning-making of educators engaging in DEIJ topics, a multidirectional conversation highlighted the purpose of collective and co-constructed narrative inquiries. Goodson and Gill (2014) illustrated the value of collective narratives and dialogue as a path for solidarity and action:

> Thus, the intention of listening, the quality of questioning, the sincerity and intensity of the attending, the purpose of the myth-making (as opposed to the scripts that society imposes on the individual), the selection of themes, and the willingness to bear witness to each other's journeys will ultimately determine one's capacity to act and react, resist the imposed script, deconstruct, reconstruct and develop autonomous space for agency. (p. 79)

While not intending to be a space for future action, the group dialogue sessions often inspired the collaborators to think of ways to make our school community more inclusive and equitable. The conversations challenged the perceptions of the school's mission and our personal educational philosophies. These dialogue sessions allowed the group members to journey alongside one another through empathetic listening and critical questioning educational spaces.

As I desired to respect their time and engagement, I was cognizant of their lives outside this co-constructed narrative study. This narrative inquiry was collaborative and driven by the learning needs of the collective group. Yet, I was prepared to support the group dialogue discussions with DEIJ content as a facilitator and resource. For some sessions, there was no guidance on my part, and collaborators brought different topics and concerns to the group for discussion. For a few sessions, I provided readings to help facilitate conversation and allowed the conversation to take shape after some initial prompting. Upon reflection, there were a couple of sessions where the conversation could have benefitted from more structure and guidance on my behalf. Still, I was consistently impressed by the questions and dialogue that naturally flowed among the group members.

Individuals and Their Experiences: One-on-One Interviews

The dialogue sessions were an opportunity to validate others' classroom and community experiences with DEIJ content and confirm their experiences with others in similar professional situations. Often, these stories bridged deep conversations among all group members, but that connection is often the exception instead of the norm. Dialogue can be challenging when set in a larger group, and while contributing members' shared input, it was not a perfectly equal conversation, as expected with natural dialogue. I conducted one-on-one interviews (Marshall & Rossman, 2016) after sessions #5 and #12 to learn about the individual collaborators' experiences in the study process. These interviews ranged from 10-to-35 minutes and expanded on different concepts from the dialogue sessions and reflections on the study process. While I am naming these as interviews, I relate to Clandinin and Connelly (2000) when they expressed:

> Interviews normally have an inequality about them. The direction of the interview, along with its specific questions, are governed by the interviewer. However, researchers who establish intimate participatory relationships with participants find it difficult, if not impossible, to conduct such interviews with participants. Even when they begin with the intention of conducting an interview, the interview often turns into a form of conversation. (p. 110)

These informal interviews consisted of questions that are, as Kim (2016) described, "open-ended, descriptive, structural, and contrast questions with which you can get to the interviewee's emotional level because they encourage more thoughtful and personally meaningful answers" (p. 170). The follow-up interviews were opportunities to learn more about the co-narrators' experiences, their likes and dislikes in the study process, and to gauge their learning and understanding. Each co-constructor engaged in two informal interviews for data consistency and validity measures.

Researcher Reflexive Journal

I practiced reflexive journaling to highlight my thoughts and ideas after the group dialogue (Leavy, 2017; Marshall & Rossman, 2016). Reflexive journaling was a way to evaluate my perspective of the dialogue and to reflect on how my bias interacted with and interrupted the conversations with my co-collaborators. As Clandinin and Connelly (2000) wrote, "Journals may, and often do, take on an intimately reflective puzzling quality, perhaps less a way to give accounts of experience . . . and more a way to puzzle out experience" (p. 103). This reflexive journal was used as a data tool as I actively participated in the conversions and research process, and it aided in my analysis of the collective stories.

Humanizing the Research

One key aspect of critical collective narrative research is the challenge of hierarchical relationships between the researcher and narrators (Clandinin & Rosiek, 2007; Hollingsworth & Dybdahl, 2007). The relationship becomes humanized by eliminating hierarchy and demonstrating effective research's complex and ever-changing nature (Cole & Knowles, 2001). The researcher acknowledges the power dynamic and continuously questions their subjectivity throughout the study (Cole & Knowles, 2001; Hollingsworth & Dybdahl, 2007). The researcher is no longer separate from the data but actively participates in how their views of narrators, contexts, and the purpose of the study influence the study design and analysis (Gavidia & Adu, 2022). In turn, a critical co-constructed narrative study focuses on establishing trust and building relationships instead of aiming to distance oneself from the potential data. Some ways to foster this dialogue and interaction include open-ended conversations and critical reflexivity on behalf of the researcher (Gavidia & Adu, 2022; Hollingsworth & Dybdahl, 2007). A critical lens also affects relationships across multiple narrators in a study. The challenge is amplifying many voices while honoring individual stories and experiences (Elbaz-Luwisch, 2007). Narrators have power over their words and agency within the study to provide feedback on the narratives shared and how they desire their stories to be represented (Gavidia & Adu, 2022; Hollingsworth & Dybdahl, 2007).

When considering data analysis in a collective and co-constructed narrative inquiry, the researcher must engage in multiple coding forms to narrow the data to categories and themes. This analysis process is dynamic and involves listening to the audio recordings of dialogue sessions multiple times, re-reading the transcripts, and layering codes. In addition to becoming well-versed and saturated in the data, collective and co-constructed narrative research benefits from data analysis conversations with a trusted colleague or advisor. As mentioned earlier in this chapter, co-constructed group dialogue sessions entail a variety of discussion topics because the collaborators determine the content and flow of conversations. Because the data is constructed collaboratively and collectively, discussing the findings with others is beneficial to illuminate overarching themes.

Disrupting Systems of Oppression and Empowering Participants

A collective and co-constructed narrative study grounded in critical inquiry ontology values stories and analysis with social and historical context and co-narrators' identities (Clandinin & Rosiek, 2007; Hollingsworth & Dybdahl, 2007). Collective narrative research can analyze large and existing capitalist structures and challenge the power constructs that continue to oppress marginalized groups. Within a critical epistemology, stories from historically marginalized populations reflect the reality of society and provide temporary experiential understandings that are historically, politically, and socially constructed (Clandinin & Rosiek, 2007; Gavidia & Adu, 2022; Hollingsworth & Dybdahl, 2007). Critical narrative research aids the narrator's agency by valuing and uplifting their stories and experiences (Clandinin & Rosiek, 2007; Hollingsworth & Dybdahl, 2007) as the "storyteller holds the position of expert of his or her own social and political location" (SooHoo, 2006, p. 16). Co-constructors or collaborators are "viewed as experts of their own local knowledge" (Berryman et al., 2013, p. 5), and the research intends to learn and understand their experiences and knowledge base.

This means that researchers acknowledge the diverse backgrounds impacting how studies are conducted and awareness of "certain voices and perspectives being privileged or marginalized within the grander narrative that holds power in society, and of how certain experiences are shaped in a particular way" (Goodson & Gill, 2014, p. 83). Challenging the historically inequitable treatment of research participants and their knowledge, collective and co-constructed narrative inquiry honors cultures, ideals, and beliefs in the research design and process. The focus shift is less on the individual and more on the collective experience, story, and meaning, as notions of "reciprocity, dialogue, and relationships building are at the core of co-creation" (Berryman et al., 2013, p. 7).

Critical Solidarity

Another key aspect of collective and co-constructed narrative inquiry is developing critical solidarity with participants. This idea goes beyond uplifting the experiences and voices of your participants to an active process of joining participants in creating positive change in their lives and the social groups they inhabit (Boucher, 2019). Solidarity can evolve in research in various ways. In some cases, critical solidarity rises out of necessity and through struggle. In other circumstances, we are forging alliances and working in community with one another toward a collective goal. Rooted in the love and protection of fellow human beings, critical solidarity emphasizes relationships and a deep connection with others to break down power structures that seek to oppress the marginalized or othered (Boucher, 2019).

"Critical solidarity means that we investigate, examine, question, challenge, and then work to dismantle power structures that are oppressing our participants, not in a way that assumes we have the answers, but as workers with our participants" (Boucher, 2019, p. 97). Examining and questioning dominant narratives and oppressive systems entail reflecting on historical contexts and searching for pathways of resistance and liberation. Boucher (2019) described solidarity as "a force that moves people, communities, and even countries to a more mutual understanding and process. It is a conscious, political stance taken to fight injustice alongside their students, their research participants, and/or their neighbors" (p. 99). Mutual understanding and care for one another solidify and humanize the relationships between researchers and participants (Boucher, 2019).

Counter-Narratives in Educational Research

In traditional narrative studies, the researcher narrates the singular lived experience of an individual and examines the story as a version of their truth. However, a critical narrative study reflects and critiques the stories shared to determine if the narrative supports or reinforces dominant narratives (Clandinin & Rosiek, 2007). These stories can represent counter-narratives that challenge the injustices that permeate various aspects of society, such as racism, sexism, and classism (Milner, 2007). SooHoo (2006) described narratives as "tools in the struggle against marginalization. They served as the vehicles for critical consciousness in that they counteracted stereotypes, provided insight into marginalization and prejudice, and uncovered social structures that perpetuate 'othering'" (p. 19). Sharing and listening to others' stories can be a transformative practice that validates the experiences of those traditionally silenced and belittled. Through this form of expression, marginalized people develop a critical awareness of their social environments and challenge normative systems.

Additionally, counter-narratives are designed to challenge historically dominant narratives regarding social and political practices that define countries such as the US and their notion of the American dream. The one-sided façade of bravado and heroism is challenged by counter-storytelling, which creates spaces for community voices to create oppositional narratives by drawing upon the experiences and lives of minority groups (Delgado, 2012). Ladson-Billings (2021) further explained the counter story as "a contrasting story that describes the story from a different vantage point . . . a way to unmoor people from received truths so that they might consider alternatives" (p. 49). Including narratives outside the dominant population allows for further understanding and various perspectives of all people involved in historical, social, and political movements. Furthermore, these stories and narratives of the "Other" are, as SooHoo (2006) explained, "the language of difference and are essential in classrooms dedicated to ongoing conversations of social justice" (p. 21). Without a comprehensive picture of everyone involved in social movements, we restrict students' critical consciousness and awareness to conjure their thoughts and opinions in classroom spaces.

Foundational Texts and Important Theorists

Collective and co-constructed narrative inquiry is a bricolage of many qualitative methods and theoretical constructs. Clandinin and Connelly (2000) explored the roots of narrative inquiry as the essence of storytelling. Stories connect people, establish relationships, and educate society on the experiences of those beyond one's community, country, or continent. The cultural, historical, and social contexts are vital for understanding stories and impact how stories express and create meaning (2000). Kim (2016) interweaves philosophical and critical theoretical concepts into narrative methods and practices, pushing this collective process to focus on conversing, connecting, and learning.

Collective and co-constructed narrative inquiry methods focus on the connections, conversations, and acts of being with others to create deep relationships rooted in collaboration, curiosity, and honor of ourselves and others (Hogg et al., 2021). Hogg et al. (2021) explored this notion of solidarity and sense of "with-ness" that "requires collective responsibility to move back and forth as we listen, seek, ponder, engage, reflect and perhaps reengage"

(p. 212). SooHoo et al. (2018) further describe the collectivity of collaborators as they listen, reflect, and engage with one another to embrace a "praxis of togetherness" (p. 133), challenging what one can imagine by themselves into the possibilities of what can be accomplished with one another.

Suggestions For Further Reading

Conle, C. (1999). Why narrative? Which narrative? Struggling with time and place in life and research. *Curriculum Inquiry, 29*(1), 7–32.

Conroy, J. C. (2004). *Betwixt & between: The liminal imagination, education, and democracy.* Peter Lang Publishing, Inc.

Crotty, M. (1998). *The foundations of social research: Meaning and perspective in the research process.* SAGE.

Darder, A. (2012). Neoliberalism in the academic borderlands: An on-going struggle for equality and human rights. *Educational Studies, 48*(5), 412–426. https://doi.org/10.1080/00131946.2012.714334

Freire, P. (1985). *The politics of education: Culture, power, and liberation.* Bergen & Garvey.

Freire, P. (2005). *Teachers as cultural workers: Letters to those who dare to teach.* Westview.

Freire, P. (2018). *Pedagogy of the oppressed.* Bloomsbury.

Freire, P. (2021a). *Pedagogy of the heart.* Bloomsbury.

Freire, P. (2021b). *Education for critical consciousness.* Bloomsbury.

Giroux, H. A., & Giroux, S. S. (2006). Challenging neoliberalism's new world order: The promise of critical pedagogy. *Cultural Studies ↔ Critical Methodologies, 6*(1), 21–32. https://doi.org/10.1177/1532708605282810

Harrison, J., Macgibbon, L., & Morton, M. (2001). Regimes of trustworthiness in qualitative research: The rigors of reciprocity. *Qualitative Inquiry, 7*(3), 323–345. http://pascal-francis.inist.fr/vibad/index.php?action=getRecordDetail&idt=14209344

hooks, b. (1994). *Teaching to transgress.* Routledge.

hooks, b. (2003). *Teaching community: A pedagogy of hope.* Routledge.

Kincheloe, J. L., McLaren, P., Steinberg, S. R., & Monzó, L. D. (2017). Critical pedagogy and qualitative research: Advancing the bricolage. In N. K. Denzin & Y. S. Lincoln (Eds.), *The SAGE handbook of qualitative research* (pp. 235–260). SAGE.

Lincoln, Y. S., Lynham, S. A., & Guba, E. G. (2011). Paradigmatic controversies, contradictions, and emerging confluences, revisited. In N. K. Denzin & Y. S. Lincoln (Eds.), *The SAGE handbook of qualitative research* (4th ed., pp. 97–128). SAGE.

Monzó, L. D., & McLaren, P. (2014). Critical pedagogy and the decolonial option: Challenges to the inevitability of capitalism. *Policy Futures in Education, 12*(4). http://dx.doi.org/10.2304/pfie.2014.12.4.513

Pinnegar, S., & Daynes, J. G. (2007). Locating narrative inquiry historically: Thematics in the turn to narrative. In D. J. Clandinin (Ed.), *Handbook of narrative inquiry: Mapping a methodology* (pp. 3–30). SAGE.

Reynolds, W. M. (2015). Critical pedagogical praxis: Risk and the hopeful struggle. In B. J. Porfilio & D. R. Ford (Eds.), *Leaders in critical pedagogy: Narratives for understanding and solidarity* (pp. 1–15). Sense Publishers.

Saldana, J. (2011). *Fundamentals of Qualitative Research.* Oxford University Press.

References

Berryman, M., SooHoo, S., & Nevin, A. (2013). *Culturally responsive methodologies.* Emerald Group Publishing Limited.

Boucher, M. L. (2019). Whose side are we on?: A call for critical solidarity with participants in education research. In V. Wang (Ed.), *Scholarly publishing and research methods across disciplines* (pp. 93–109). IGI Global. https://doi.org/10.4018/978/1/5225/7730/0.ch005

Broadhurst, C., Locke, L. A., & Ardoin, S. (2021). "Leading from the middle": Exploring stories of women working for change in PK–12 schools. *The Professional Educator, 44*(1), 8–20. https://doi-org.libproxy.chapman.edu/10.47038/tpe.44.01.04

Clandinin, D. J., & Connelly, F. M. (2000). *Narrative inquiry: Experience and story in qualitative research.* Josey-Bass.

Clandinin, D. J., & Rosiek, J. (2007). Mapping a landscape of narrative inquiry: Borderland spaces and tensions. In D. J. Clandinin (Ed.), *Handbook of narrative inquiry: Mapping a methodology* (pp. 35–51). SAGE.

Cole, A. L., & Knowles, J. G. (2001). *Lives in context.* AltaMira Press.

Delgado, R. (2012). *Critical race theory: An introduction.* New York University Press.

Elbaz-Luwisch, F. (2007). Studying teachers' lives and experience: Narrative inquiry into K–12 teaching. In D. J. Clandinin (Ed.), *Handbook of narrative inquiry: Mapping a methodology* (pp. 357–382). SAGE.

Gavidia, L. A. P., & Adu, J. (2022). Critical narrative inquiry: An examination of a methodological approach. *International Journal of Qualitative Methods, 21.* https://doi-org.libproxy.chapman.edu/10.1177/16094069221081594

Goodson, I., & Gill, S. (2014). *Critical narrative as pedagogy.* Bloomsbury.

Hogg, L., & Achieng-Evensen, C., & Stockbridge, K., & SooHoo, S. (2021). Pedagogies of with-ness: Reflecting on and beyond the exhibition. In L. Hogg, K. Stockbridge, C. Achieng-Evensen, & S. SooHoo (Eds.), *Pedagogies of with-ness: Students, teachers, voice and agency* (pp. 211–216). Myers Education Press.

Hollingsworth, S., & Dybdahl, M. (2007).Talking to learn: The critical role of conversation in narrative inquiry. In D. J. Clandinin (Ed.), *Handbook of narrative inquiry: Mapping a methodology* (pp. 146–167). SAGE.

Kim, J-H. (2016). *Understanding narrative inquiry: The crafting and analysis of stories as research.* SAGE.

Ladson-Billings, G. (2021). *Critical race theory in education: A scholar's journey.* Multicultural Education Series.

Latta, M., & Kim, J-H. (2011). Investing in the curricular lives of educators: Narrative inquiry as pedagogical medium. *Journal of Curriculum Studies, 43*(5), 679–695. http://doi.org/10.1080.00220272.2011.609566

Leavy, P. (2017). *Research design: Quantitative, qualitative, mixed-methods, arts-based, and community-based participatory research approaches.* Guilford Press.

Lewis, P. J., & Adeney, R. (2014). Narrative research. In J. Mills & M. Birks (Eds.), *Qualitative methodology: A practical guide* (pp. 161–179). SAGE

Marshall, C., & Rossman, G. (2016). *Designing qualitative research.* SAGE.

Milner IV, H. R. (2007). Race, narrative inquiry, and self-study in curriculum and teacher education. *Education and Urban Society, 39*(4), 584–609. http://doi.org/10.1177/0013124507301577

Roady, N. N. (2024). Progress is progress: A collective narrative inquiry exploring the experiences of social justice educators in a private, PK–eighth grade school [Doctoral dissertation]. Chapman University. https://doi.org/10.36837/chapman.000621

SooHoo, S. (2006). *Talking leaves: Narratives of otherness.* Hampton Press.

Chapter 13 Discussion Questions

1. How does collective narrative inquiry differ from traditional qualitative research methods, and in what ways does it seek to disrupt hierarchical relationships between researchers and participants? What are the implications of this approach for fostering critical solidarity and empowering participants?
2. In what ways can artifacts such as articles, books, podcasts, or art contribute to dialogue sessions in collective narrative research? How do these artifacts facilitate deeper connections and understanding among participants, particularly in the context of DEIJ work?
3. Reflect on the challenges and potential limitations of co-constructed dialogue sessions in collective narrative inquiry. How can researchers balance the need for structure with the goal of fostering organic, multidirectional conversations that honor participants' voices?
4. The essay highlights the importance of counter-narratives in challenging dominant societal structures. How can educators and researchers use collective narrative inquiry to amplify counter-narratives and advocate for systemic change in educational contexts?

FOURTEEN

Disrupting Power Through Photo Elicitation: Centering Participants in Research

Michael L. Boucher, Jr.

PHOTO ELICITATION USES PHOTOGRAPHS TO elicit participant responses during the data-gathering phase of a study. While used most often in qualitative work, there are many ways to approach using photos in research. As a general technique, photo methods can empower participants, allowing them to gain new perspectives, new theorization by participants, deeper understanding, richer, more consequential data, and insightful new perceptions for the participants (Boucher, 2018a; b). Examples of photo methods represented in the literature are most often one of the following:

a) The participants take the photos and present them and their meanings to the researcher.
b) The participants are involved in another project that involves photography, and the photos are used to interpret their experiences with the project.
c) The participant or the researcher takes pictures that no one but the researcher and participant see.

This method's flexibility allows a researcher committed to ethical work with participants to create meaningful studies without demanding a specific theoretical framework. When the researcher seeks to do justice and empower the participants in a study, photo methods can decenter the researcher as the questioner and center the participant as the inventor and creator of her/his/their story. This technique can also lead to insightful new perceptions for the researcher and participant.

Although there are many variations of photo methods, the general process described by Torre and Murphy (2015) includes the following steps:

1. Researchers develop a topic for investigation.
2. Researchers identify participants and invite them to the study.
3. Researchers or participants take photographs relevant to the research question or topic.
4. After the photos are downloaded, the researcher uses them to guide interviews and elicit responses.
5. The data is analyzed, and findings are reported.

A key strength of photo elicitation lies in its ability to spark powerful, emotionally resonant conversations during interviews. By using photographs as prompts, researchers can evoke reflective responses that go beyond surface-level dialogue. Typically, participants are shown an image and asked a simple yet profound question—"*What is happening in this photo?*"—which often initiates a rich and layered conversation. This one question begins the discussion that can reveal theories, history, and reflection beyond what is often possible in a traditional interview. For example, when working with adolescents, asking a teen a question is a revolutionary endeavor. Teens are seldom asked for their ideas and opinions and are even less often asked to teach adults about their world. That is one of the great reveals when using this method. Often, the participant will explain that no one has ever asked them to explain their lives, and this research gives them the space to reflect and think about the phenomenon captured in that photo (see Gallo, 2002).

Photographs can enhance ethnographic research in numerous ways, allowing the researcher to better understand a participant's truth. Traditionally, ethnography involves the ethnographer living among the people being studied, gathering data through observation, self-reporting, and interviews (Carspecken, 1996; Creswell, 2012). However, one possible weakness is that the researcher risks seeing only what they expect or desire to see without intermediaries to challenge the researcher's biases and perceptions. Photo methods can enhance these traditional approaches and broaden the scope of data collection by revealing participants' lived truths (Bridger, 2013; Crilly et al., 2006; Leonard & McKnight, 2014; Prosser & Loxley, 2007; Shaw, 2013; Zartler & Richter, 2012). In studies using photographs, the images serve as an intermediary between researcher and participant, helping to avoid the *inspecting gaze*, as Foucault (1980) described. Photographs help reduce participants' self-consciousness, create a more comfortable interview setting, and encourage them to reveal deeper insights about their lives, practices, and space. Most importantly, participants become *collaborators* rather than *subjects* under examination. They are empowered to reflect on their experiences through the lens of the images.

Crilly et al. (2006) explained that photo elicitation in interviews leads to data that is "difficult to achieve by verbal exchanges alone. . . . This is because such stimuli bring factors external to the interview situation into view, prompting a response to 'not now' moments, 'not here' events, and 'not present' actors" (pp. 341–342). Images introduce external factors, prompting participants to respond to moments, events, and individuals not immediately present in the interview setting. By engaging with the photos, participants naturally theorize about their meaning. For example, in studies where the researcher provides the photographs, participants can respond to these images as though they were reacting to a traditional interview question, yet their focus shifts away from the researcher, leading to unexpected insights (Boucher, 2014, 2018a; Boucher & Helfenbein, 2015). When a constructive relationship has been built between the researcher and the participant, participants feel more comfortable discussing challenging topics without seeking approval from the researcher (Walton & Niblett, 2013).

Disrupting Systems of Oppression and Empowering Participants

Historically, ethnography has been associated with oppressive and voyeuristic research methods. However, critical ethnography shifts the focus toward an ethical commitment to uplifting communities and creating opportunities for participant empowerment. This approach aligns with a model of solidarity that emphasizes relational ethics in research by fostering collaborative relationships that resist power imbalances and prioritizing the voices of marginalized participants (Boucher, 2018a, 2018b, 2019). This type of solidarity requires researchers to move beyond surface-level allyship to a deeper, ongoing commitment to dismantling systemic inequities and amplifying the lived experiences of those often silenced in traditional research (Boucher, 2018a). When participants contribute photographs, these images reveal their lived experiences in ways that verbal interviews alone cannot capture. This framework underscores the importance of this co-creative process, where participants are empowered as equal partners, shaping the data and interpreting and disseminating research findings. This approach ensures that research outputs are not merely about the participants but also for and with them, fostering *critical solidarity* (Boucher, 2019).

Integrating a critical perspective into research methods is a transformative and essential endeavor, reshaping our understanding of qualitative inquiry. Carspecken (1996) emphasized that in critical social research, "we immediately translate truth claims into validity claims, understanding that some of the content of any truth claim is going to be culturally bound" (p. 57). This perspective rejects the notion of absolute or universal truths. Instead, critical researchers align with pragmatists, accepting that "any assertion will always be fallible" (p. 57). This fallibility is not a weakness but a strength, as it acknowledges the complexity and cultural specificity inherent in human experiences.

Madison (2012) further highlighted the role of reflexivity in critical ethnography, describing it as a process in which researchers hold themselves accountable for their interpretations and positionalities. She noted that reflexive ethnography demands a self-critical lens, which is particularly vital when engaging with sensitive topics such as race in America. This reflexivity also extends to understanding what defines a successful teacher, as it compels researchers to consider their biases and the cultural contexts of their inquiries (p. 7).

Rather than striving for definitive conclusions, critical researchers embrace the human fallibility that Carspecken argued enhances the reliability of qualitative and critical research. By doing so, they recognize that "when dealing with people, there is never just one undeniable answer," allowing researchers to represent participants' humanity with greater authenticity (Boucher, 2018a, p. 209). Thomas (1993) encapsulated this perspective by describing critical ethnography as a metaphor that "conveys a particular social imaginary" (p. 20). This framework challenges existing structures and envisions new possibilities, emphasizing the transformative potential of critical inquiry in education and beyond.

For instance, Gallo (2002) conducted an autodocumentary project in which immigrant and refugee workers were given cameras to document how they found meaning in their work. The study, aimed at teaching English and advocating for workers' rights, allowed participants to reclaim their narratives. Gallo explained, "Too often they [immigrant workers] are ignored or belittled; portrayed as exotic, pitiable or comic. Therefore, it becomes an empowering exercise to show themselves through their own visual perspectives as multifaceted individuals expressing their joys and concerns" (p. 52). The photographs not only provided scientifically valuable data but also empowered the workers by allowing them to depict their realities.

Similarly, Allen (2011) utilized participant photographs in her study, which employed photo diaries to explore how teens navigated their sexual lives and how these experiences unfolded in school settings. According to Allen, photographs facilitated deeper discussions with participants, as "photos offer a sense of space and therefore insights about the spatial dimensions of sexuality which are abstract and less easily accessed through talk alone" (p. 488). These examples underscore how photographs allow participants to bring the world outside the research into the study, ensuring they retain control over their narratives.

Critical ethnographers must remain conscious of the power dynamics embedded in the images and the equipment used to create them. Tools such as iPads, cameras, and other digital devices may be inaccessible to disadvantaged participants, raising equity concerns. Researchers must be mindful of the ethical implications of providing equipment participants could not otherwise afford. As with all qualitative research, power relations and the researcher's positionality need careful examination. The researcher's duty is to earn participants' trust, ensuring that their stories and images are treated with the respect they deserve.

The treatment of participants, their stories, and their images directly reflect a researcher's integrity. Luttrell (2010) emphasized the need to include participants as co-researchers rather than mere subjects: "a self-conscious effort to incorporate [participating children] as producers, interpreters, circulators, exhibitors and social analysts of their own and each other's images" (p. 234). Empowering participants as co-researchers requires handling their narratives and images with care, allowing for critique where necessary but avoiding the imposition of the researcher's interpretations over those of the participants. Photographs foster co-research relationships in a non-threatening way, enabling participants to share and analyze their data collaboratively. As Luttrell (2010) further suggested, "We also need projects that open up opportunities to unsettle, fragment or dislodge other's gazes—if only for moments in time where young people can see themselves and be seen by others in alternative ways" (p. 234). Photographs become valuable tools in critical ethnography by creating a space for mutual understanding and shared experiences.

Nevertheless, critiques exist regarding photo methods, particularly in research aimed at empowering participants. Prosser et al. (2008) emphasized that consent is not a one-time event but an ongoing process, requiring permission at every stage, from creating to displaying images. Similarly, Wang and Redwood-Jones (2001) warned that not all legally permissible photography practices are ethical. For example, while photographing and distributing images of people in public spaces may be legally allowed, ethical concerns arise when photographers assign "meaning" to these images without explicit consent. This issue is especially significant when working with vulnerable populations, such as children, where power imbalances can prevent them from being complete and equal partners in the research process.

Foundational Texts and Theorists

Douglas Harper (2002) reintroduced the concept of photo elicitation to a new generation of researchers, making a case for its use in ethnographic research. He theorized that photographs are more comforting and engaging for participants because they stimulate different areas of the brain compared to verbal exchanges. Harper argued that the emotional impact of images varies along a continuum, from the most scientific, such as inventories of artifacts, to the most intimate, such as personal family portraits. The type of photograph used directly affects the level of emotional engagement, with intimate images revealing more about participants' internal struggles than would scientific or detached images.

In educational research, Marisol Clark-Ibáñez has been a prominent figure in using photo elicitation. Her work highlights how photographs can free the researcher to capture the authentic voices of children, who may not express their thoughts through traditional techniques such as journaling (Clark-Ibáñez, 2004, 2008). She explained, "Using researcher-produced photographs is an excellent way to conduct theory-driven research. Researcher-photographers may capture taken-for-granted aspects of the participants' community or life that prompt discussion" (p. 1509). However, she cautioned that researchers may also miss essential aspects of participants' lives if they rely solely on their own perspectives.

Clark-Ibáñez (2004) further pointed out that photo elicitation, especially with children, can lead to greater investment in the research process. Traditional clipboard-style interviews often result in brief, surface-level responses. By contrast, photo elicitation can foster more in-depth engagement, as participants are either eager to share the photos they have taken or curious to see what the researcher has captured.

In conclusion, using photographs in research, particularly within critical ethnography, offers a powerful method for disrupting systems of oppression and empowering participants. Visual methods such as photo elicitation allow individuals to represent their lived experiences on their terms, offering insights that traditional interviews alone may not capture. By enabling participants to maintain control over their narratives, these methods foster deeper engagement and co-researcher relationships, as seen in the work of scholars including Gallo, Allen, and Luttrell. However, researchers must remain mindful of power dynamics, positionality, and the accessibility of the tools provided. Ultimately, incorporating images promotes a richer, more inclusive understanding of participants' realities, positioning photography as a vital tool for challenging dominant perspectives and amplifying marginalized voices.

Suggestions for Further Reading

Briggs, L. P., Stedman, R. C., & Krasny, M. E. (2014). Photo-elicitation methods in studies of children's sense of place. *Children, Youth and Environments, 24*(3), 153. https://doi.org/10.7721/chilyoutenvi.24.3.0153

Hamilton, E. R. (2016). Picture this: Multimodal representations of prospective teachers' metaphors about teachers and teaching. *Teaching and Teacher Education, 55*, 33–44. https://doi.org/10.1016/j.tate.2015.12.007

O'Brien, D. (2013). Visual Research with young d/Deaf people: An investigation of the transitional experiences of d/Deaf young people from mainstream schools using auto-driven photo-elicitation interviews. *Graduate Journal of Social Science, 10*(2), 152–175.

Ruto-Korir, R., & Lubbe-De Beer, C. (2012). The potential for using visual elicitation in understanding preschool teachers' beliefs of appropriate educational practices. *South African Journal of Education, 32*(4), 393–405.

Shaw, P. A. (2020). Photo-elicitation and photo-voice: Using visual methodological tools to engage with younger children's voices about inclusion in education. *International Journal of Research & Method in Education, 44*(4), 337–351.

Stocknall, N., & Davis, S. (2011). Uncovering pre-service teacher beliefs about young children: A photographic elicitation methodology. *Issues in Educational Research*, (21), 192–209.

Taylor, E. W. (2002). Using still photography in making meaning of adult educators' teaching beliefs. *Studies in the Education of Adults, 34*(2), 123–139.

Walls, J., & Holquist, S. E. (2019). Through their eyes, in their words: Using photo-elicitation to amplify student voice in policy and school improvement research. In K. K. Strunk & L. A. Locke (Eds.), *Research Methods for Social Justice and Equity in Education* (pp. 151–161). Springer.

References

Allen, L. (2011). "Picture this": Using photo-methods in research on sexualities and schooling. *Qualitative Research, 11*(5), 487–504.

Boucher, M. L. (2014). More than an ally: A successful white teacher who builds solidarity with his African American students. *Urban Education, 51*(1), 82–107.

Boucher, M. L., & Helfenbein, R. J. (2015). The push and the pull: Deficit models, Ruby Payne, and becoming a "Warm Demander." *The Urban Review, 47*(4), 742–758.

Boucher, M. L. (Ed.). (2018a). *Participant empowerment through photo elicitation in ethnographic education research: New research and approaches.* Springer. http://doi.org/10.1007/978-3-319-64413-4

Boucher, M. L. (2018b). Troubling empowerment. In Boucher, M. L., (Ed.) *Participant empowerment through photo elicitation in ethnographic education research: New research and approaches* (pp. 227–234). Springer.

Boucher, M. L. (2019). Whose side are we on?: A call for critical solidarity with participants in education research. In V. Wang, *Scholarly publishing and research methods across disciplines* (pp. 93–109). IGI Global.

Bridger, L. (2013). Seeing and telling households: A case for photo elicitation and graphic elicitation in qualitative research. *Graduate Journal of Social Science, 10*(2), 106–131.

Carspecken, P. F. (1996). *Critical ethnography in educational research: A theoretical and practical guide.* Routledge.

Clark- Ibáñez, M. K. (2004). Framing the social world with photo-elicitation interviews. *American Behavioral Scientist, 47*(12), 1507–1527.

Clark-Ibáñez, M. K. (2008). Gender and being "bad": Inner city students' photographs. In P. Thompson (Ed.), *Doing Visual Research with Children and Young People* (pp. 95–113). Routledge.

Creswell, J. W. (2012). *Qualitative inquiry and research design: Choosing among five approaches* (3rd ed.). SAGE.

Crilly, N., Blackwell, A. F., & Clarkson, P. J. (2006). Graphic elicitation: Using research diagrams as interview stimuli. *Qualitative Research, 6*(3), 341–366.

Foucault, M. (1980). *Power-knowledge: Selected interviews and other writings, 1972–1977* (5th ed.). Pantheon.

Gallo, M. L. (2002). Picture this: Immigrant workers use photography for communication and change. *Journal of Workplace Learning, 14*(2), 49–57.

Harper, D. (2002). Talking about pictures: A case for photo elicitation. *Visual Studies, 17*(1), 13–26.

Leonard, M., & McKnight, M. (2014). Look and tell: Using photo-elicitation methods with teenagers. *Children's Geographies, 13*(6), 629–642.

Luttrell, W. (2010). "A camera is a big responsibility": A lens for analysing children's visual voices. *Visual Studies, 25*(3), 224–237.

Madison, D. S. (2012). *Critical ethnography: Method, ethics, and performance* (2nd ed.). SAGE.

Prosser, J., & Loxley, A. (2007). Enhancing the contribution of visual methods to inclusive education. *Journal of Research in Special Educational Needs, 7*(1), 55–68.

Prosser, J., Clark, A., & Wiles, R. (2008). *Visual research ethics at the crossroads.* Working paper #10. https://hummedia.manchester.ac.uk/schools/soss/morgancentre/research/wps/10-2008-11-realities-prosseretal.pdf

Shaw, D. (2013). A new look at an old research method: Photo-elicitation. *TESOL Journal, 4*(4), 785–799.

Thomas, J. (1993). *Doing critical ethnography.* SAGE.

Torre, D., & Murphy, J. (2015). A different lens: Changing perspectives using photo-elicitation interviews. *Education policy analysis archives, 23*, 111. https://doaj.org/article/c7bdbb8ddf81470f900b8141ecb120a4

Walton, G., & Niblett, B. (2013). Investigating the problem of bullying through photo elicitation. *Journal of Youth Studies, 16*(5), 646–662.

Wang, C. C., & Redwood-Jones, Y. A. (2001). Photovoice ethics: Perspectives from Flint photovoice. *Health Education & Behavior, 28*(5), 560–572. https://doi.org/10.1177/109019810102800504

Zartler, U., & Richter, R. (2012). My family through the lens. Photo interviews with children and sensitive aspects of family life. *Children & Society, 28*(1), 42–54.

Chapter 14 Discussion Questions

1. How does the use of photo elicitation disrupt traditional power dynamics in research, particularly within critical ethnography? Provide examples from the text or your own experience where this method may empower participants or challenge systemic inequities.
2. What are the ethical implications of using participant-generated photographs in research? Discuss the role of consent and positionality in photo elicitation and propose strategies researchers can employ to address potential power imbalances and ethical concerns.
3. How does reflexivity play a role in successfully implementing photo elicitation in critical ethnography? Analyze how researchers can balance their interpretations with participants' narratives to ensure an ethical and authentic co-research relationship.
4. Considering examples such as Gallo's (2002) work with immigrant workers and Allen's (2011) study with teens, how can photo elicitation be applied to educational settings to enhance understanding of students' lived experiences? What challenges might arise, and how could researchers address these in practice?

FIFTEEN

Conclusion: Catalytic Validity and the Praxis of Critical Research

Zachary A. Casey

PRAXIS MIGHT BE ONE OF the most misunderstood concepts we have in the critical scholarly tradition. In our field of educational research, we most often associate the concept of praxis with the work of Paulo Freire (2000), who gave us the most lasting definition of the foundationally Marxist concept: praxis means action and reflection in equal measure on the world to transform it. When we encounter this concept, perhaps in *Pedagogy of the Oppressed* (1970/2000) or perhaps in other works influenced by critical pedagogy more broadly, there is a strong tendency to understand *praxis*, meaning that action and reflection must occur simultaneously to constitute an authentic praxis. In order to be engaged in praxis, one must be engaged in a reflexive activity while also working to materially impact reality at one and the same time, all together, all the time. Is this actually possible?

Certainly, supposing one is focused and engaged in the full force of critical activity. In that case, they likely cannot also be thinking deeply about the ways their work is always-already partial and thus responding to oppression in ways that privilege certain things while marginalizing others (Kumashiro, 2002). Such reflection can be found where it happens, in the before and after of activity. If we must act-reflect and reflect-act all together all the time, we are likely to generate a stasis and thus an acquiescence to the status quo. This makes critical research projects and methodologies as developed and detailed in this volume practically impossible. Thus, we need strategies to avoid such traps in our work that are relevant across different and even competing notions of what is meant by qualitative research, especially those projects aiming to be disruptive and seeking to advance the project of humanization and human flourishing.

The action side of praxis is not meant to be imagined primarily as a research activity. While certainly the work of collecting data should and likely must be an *active* one, the action on the side of humanization that we are struggling for is advancing the life chances and outcomes for historically marginalized people. It is rare that this work overlaps completely and neatly with the demands of rigorous and scholarly qualitative inquiry. We are thus hailed to think of our critical research work in instrumentalist ways (Horkheimer, 2004). The point of our work is not in the work itself but rather in what it makes available or how it can be put to use. Studying oppression does not act on said oppression directly unless such study moves beyond the traditionally positivistic research rituals of the disinterested and "objective" observer and instead functions as a *catalyst*, something that causes a change.

This is precisely what the critical feminist concept of *catalytic validity* is meant to work towards. As developed by Patti Lather (1991), catalytic validity challenges traditional positivistic notions of validity as anchored in mathematical certainty amid scales of reliability in statistical contexts. Lather tells us, "Catalytic validity represents the degree to which the research process re-orients, focuses and energizes participants toward knowing reality in order to transform it, a process Freire (1973/2000)[1] terms conscientization" (Lather, 1991, p. 68). Freirean conscientization, *conscientização*, means "learning to perceive social, political, and economic contradictions, and to take action against the oppressive elements of reality" (Freire, 2000, p. 35). Conscientization refers to the process of learning in ways that generate and move towards praxis, which focuses our attention on the most salient and hegemonic components that determine life chances for social actors. Freire's insistence on understanding the contradictions that are ever-present in our reality offers a pedagogical project of teaching and learning that is working toward transformation—not only learning about injustice or learning how to conceptualize something as unjust but learning in ways that work toward responding, in a material sense, to the injustice we are collectively focused on in our dialogic work of teaching and learning with and for one another.

Catalytic validity is present when our research has gone beyond the instrumentalist quality of working for us in a careerist sense, as is often the case in so-called extractive sorts of research projects. In such moments, the researcher is imagined as a fly-in, fly-out social actor, someone who is there to document and record and then leave to go code and write up the results in ways that, at best, can indirectly support the work of those being studied. Whether we refer to those we are working with as *participants* or *subjects* makes no difference if the subjectivity we regard them with begins and ends with their role in our research. All social actors exist in intersecting systems of oppression and wildly complex histories of dispossession, alienation, and ideological coercion (Crenshaw, 1991; hooks, 1994; Thandeka, 2006; Casey, 2016). If we objectify them as a *population* to be "studied" and nothing more, regardless of the humanizing intentions of our work, we are functioning on the side of domination and oppression. For our research to have catalytic validity, it must work on the side of humanizing change and transformation by changing those who participate in the research process.

This change is not primarily figured as living in the researcher. While Lather (1991) insists that authentically postpositivist research changes those who take it up, catalytic validity centers the subjects of research, the *researched.* She wrote:

> The argument for catalytic validity lies not only within the recognition of the reality-altering impact of the research process but also in the desire to consciously channel this impact so that *respondents* gain self-understanding and, ultimately, self-determination through research participation. (*my emphasis*, p. 68)

Our work has catalytic validity when participating in it changes those who do participate in ways that enable greater "self-understanding" and "self-determination." This has nothing whatsoever to do with the ultimate venue where such research is presented and shared. Catalytic validity is not found by analyzing impact factors of journals or weighing citation counts for a particular academic press. *Where* the research is disseminated has nothing to do with what participating in it meant and activated for the participants, for those being studied. The call is thus for researchers to understand the impact of their/our work not in terms of the ways such work is rewarded or punished in the academy but rather by what it does for the folks we are most concerned with and for, the people generous enough to work with us in our research projects.

Lather (1991) tells us that catalytic validity "flies directly in the face of the positivist demand for researcher neutrality" (p. 68). This resonates deeply with the Freirean (1973/2000) insistence that there is no apolitical or disinterested form of teaching and learning possible—all pedagogy is always already political because it represents choices among competing conceptions of the good, the just, and the worthy. The very same is true of any and all research activity: Even *objectivity* is itself a form of bias. That we will always be engaged in politically charged work, thus calls on us, especially as qualitative researchers, to articulate for ourselves and others what our desires actually consist of, such as we are able to articulate them (Ellsworth, 1997), and why. The qualitative trope of explaining to readers who we are and how we identify as researchers is essential not because it offers readers a way of reading past our relative positionalities and biases but precisely because our work can only ever be comprehended as in conversation with who we are and how we move in the world. As political beings, we are always responding to and acting in and on political contexts. We possess the possibility to make such potential slippages and difficulties for our scholarly work into part of what constitutes the work itself, and we can be guided in what this entails if we follow Lather's insights into centering the experiences and agency of our research participants above and beyond any other set of concerns.

In my own work, these commitments have seen me work primarily with others who identify in similar ways to me: I'm a white teacher, and my qualitative work has focused almost exclusively on understanding the antiracist contexts and contradictions for other folks who identify as white and work in schools (Casey, 2015; McManimon & Casey, 2018; Casey & McManimon, 2020, as a few examples). My identifications as cis-male, middle classed, partnered, a parent, from the US, a stage 4 cancer survivor, and so on are all part of my analyses even when I am not immediately focused on each or every particular component of my identity and subjectivity. Presenting these elements of who I am as part of the analysis I am offering works in multiple directions—it is not doing only one thing, nor is it merely a perfunctory disclosure so that I might move quickly to the relevant and more salient components of whatever it is I am keen to present to others. This, of course, is not meant to function as a call to narrowly "study your own kind" or some other kind of reactionary and anti-intellectual directive, but rather a reminder that one brings all of themselves and all of their past experiences with them into any and every social encounter. Working through such entanglements provides potential connections and scaffolds for our participants. These opportunities enable them to benefit from collaboration with us in ways aligned with Lather's (1991) emphasis on advancing their *self-determination* and *self-understanding.*

I would argue that these conscientizing outcomes—arising from participants' engagement in research with researchers—have the potential to foster collective and shared experiences. Such outcomes extend beyond individual gains, creating a broader sense of shared understanding and growth (Casey, 2025). Still, we must nuance this further because there is a taken-for-granted automaticity at play in a surface-level engagement with catalytic validity that must be addressed before proceeding.

It is not the case that I can always know, ahead of time, what the experience of my participants will be in their engagement(s) with me. A story from a study I conducted while living in South Africa comes to mind as an example of how catalytic validity cannot always be guaranteed ahead of time or even fully understood. I used a form of snowball sampling (Browne, 2005) to recruit participants for an interview study. I was interested in understanding how white practicing teachers understood their racial identities as impacting their work in the schools and classrooms in which they worked (Casey, 2015). While many insist on the relative benefit for those historically understood as racially privileged to reflect deeply on their/our racial identities and how whiteness impacts their/our lives and work (Thandeka, 2006; Lowenstein, 2009; Jupp et al., 2016; Tatum, 2017; Casey & McManimon, 2020; etc.), the idea that such engagements are always-already generative and helpful must be challenged. The first few white teachers I was able to speak with reported how much our conversations meant to them. They thanked me for helping them think more deeply about elements of their work or lives, and some even signaled that our interview had inspired them to do or try something new in their classrooms that they saw as working to combat white supremacy and systemic oppressions. In snowball sampling, participants help to recruit others—I was thus able to find folks willing to work with me in large part because of the relatively positive experiences some of my early participants reported having in their interviews with me. Today, almost 15 years later, I most vividly remember the only interaction that did not feel as though it was helpful to my participant.

We spent less than ten minutes together. After I bought us coffees and we found a seat at the café, I asked her to tell me her teacher story: how she came to be a teacher and where she had spent time in school as both a teacher and student. After this, I asked about the racial contexts she worked in, and her tone and affect immediately shifted. When I tried to explain more about what I meant, she stood up abruptly and pushed in her chair. She told me, half yelling, "My learners are five and six years old, they don't know anything about race, they don't think about race, and so I don't either. Race has nothing to do with anything I do. You're just making it out, so I look racist." And with that, she took one last quick sip of her drink and left. I turned off the recorder, wondered what to do with her signed consent form, and questioned whether or not I should include her in the number of teachers I spoke with that would make up my eventual "study" as I worked to continue my research.

I think my project had a great deal of catalytic validity for most of my participants. Of course, it is not actually up to me and represents a form of unknowability (Kumashiro, 2015) that is endemic to the very nature of qualitative research. I am only ever able to give limited interpretations. I do not have any direct way of testing or measuring what happened as a result of speaking with me in the case of these white South African teachers. Even if I did, we would not be able to neatly delineate those aspects of their work and the outcomes for their students that followed from it in ways that would clearly point to my contributions as such. The humbling result is that catalytic validity is ultimately not determined by the researcher—it is not up to us—but rather by the researched. And it is not always the case that everyone who participates will have the same kinds of experiences and thus end up engaging in the same sorts of changes and transformations. Our work is thus always-already partial, regardless of the length of time we spend in the "field" or the relative depth of our engagement. Perhaps the kindergarten teacher I spoke with thought more about our interaction after speaking with her colleagues and classmates who connected me with her. Maybe not.

The methods described and detailed in this volume offer numerous pathways and lines of flight to engage with and in our world in ways that offer at least the possibility of working on the side of human flourishing and humanization. However, they do not give us clear directions on how to realize the transformations we wish to see in the world. Methods are thus instrumental concepts: They are tools to be used, and while all such tools come replete with cultural histories and ideological baggage, they can be put to use in ways that work against structural oppressions or in ways that reinforce such oppressions (Horkheimer, 2004). Sometimes, projects do both at the same time, as focus and attention on any one particular thing is simultaneously a lack of focus and attention on everything else (Kumashiro, 2002). Research methods work to help us with *how* to study, but not *what* or *whom* we ought to be studying.

Research has a long and troubled history of functioning as yet more evidence of harm in the lives of historically marginalized peoples. There are far too many research studies that merely repeat past findings of the same old oppressions (Cross, 2005). As Marxist geographer, David Harvey (2020) has written:

> Mapping even more evidence of man's patent inhumanity to man is actually counterproductive in the sense that it allows the bleeding-heart liberal in us to pretend that we are contributing to a solution when, in fact, we are not. (para 21)

While Harvey's patriarchal framing here deserves careful criticism—using *man* to stand in for all people functions in citationally oppressive ways—his point is critically significant for the present discussion. Our research interventions will not advance the project of humanization if they merely function to further document and record ever more evidence of oppression. We know very well who is suffering in our world and communities. Our task as researchers with desires to be transformative is to do more with our work than to simply repeat the same old findings of white supremacist capitalist [hetero]patriarchy (hooks, 1994). Catalytic validity offers us an aim and goal that can help us push past the forces that compel us back into repeating the same kinds of studies that generate the same kinds of findings that function to leave the status quo unchecked and unchanged, albeit better defined and updated with the most current data.

The praxis of critical research is thus a series of works and thoughts, actions, and reflections in dialectical tension that do not always happen in the exact same moment but can be said to be happening at the same time if we allow ourselves the temporal permission to regard our efforts in terms of their humanizing potential rather than their quantifiable qualities. My scholarly engagements must be anchored in rich explorations of history and culture, even as I seek to work on and respond to these legacies of dispossession and oppression that determine so much of our contemporary reality in concrete material ways. The concepts in this book offer many different pathways and approaches for critical researchers—the challenge now, however, is to make these tools function in ways that grow our collective capacity in the always-unfinished project of becoming more fully human.

Note

1. Here Lather is referencing *Pedagogy of the Oppressed*. My copy is from 2000, and thus I hope the reader will not be thrown off by my clarifying Lather's point with what might appear as a different Freirean citation than the one she is making. Later versions of Freire's work, including the one I mobilize throughout this essay, have been edited to be more inclusive in terms of gendered concepts. The original text, partially because it was translated out of the original Portuguese, used male pronouns almost exclusively. Thus, I am citing the same book here as Lather, just a more contemporary edition.

Suggestions for Further Reading and References

Browne, K. (2005). Snowball sampling: Using social networks to research non-heterosexual women. *International Journal of Social Research Methodology, 8*(1), 47–60.

Casey, Z. A. (2015). Strict fathers, competing culture (s), and racialized poverty: White South African teachers' conceptions of themselves as racialized actors. *Race Ethnicity and Education, 19*(6), 1262–1274.

Casey, Z. A. (2016). *A pedagogy of anticapitalist antiracism: Whiteness, neoliberalism, and resistance in education.* State University of New York Press.

Casey, Z. A. (2025). *Critical pedagogy and the trouble with consciousness raising.* Routledge.

Casey, Z. A., & McManimon, S. K. (2020). *Building pedagogues: White practicing teachers and the struggle for antiracist work in schools.* State University of New York Press.

Crenshaw, K. (1991). Race, gender, and sexual harassment. *s. Cal. l. Rev., 65*, 1467.

Cross, B. E. (2005). New racism, reformed teacher education, and the same ole' oppression. *Educational Studies, 38*(3), 263–274.

Ellsworth, E. (1997). *Teaching positions: Difference, pedagogy, and the power of address.* Teachers College Press.

Freire, P. (2000). *Pedagogy of the oppressed.* Continuum.

Freire, P. (2006). *Teachers as cultural workers: Letters to those who dare teach.* Westview.

Harvey, D. (2020, June 2). *Capitalism is not the solution to urban America's problems—Capitalism itself is the problem.* Jacobin. https://jacobin.com/2020/06/david-harvey-cities-capital-labor-crisis

hooks, b. (1994). *Teaching to transgress: Education as the practice of freedom.* Routledge.

Horkheimer, M. (2004). *Eclipse of reason.* Continuum.

Jupp, J. C., Berry, T. R., & Lensmire, T. J. (2016). Second-wave white teacher identity studies: A review of white teacher identity literatures from 2004 through 2014. *Review of Educational Research, 86*(4), 1151–1191.

Kumashiro, K. K. (2002). *Troubling education:" Queer" activism and anti-oppressive pedagogy.* Routledge.

Kumashiro, K. K. (2015). *Against common sense: Teaching and learning toward social justice.* Routledge.

Lather, P. (1991). *Getting smart: Feminist research and pedagogy within/in the postmodern*. Routledge.

Lowenstein, K. L. (2009). The work of multicultural teacher education: Reconceptualizing white teacher candidates as learners. *Review of Educational Research, 79*(1), 163–196.

McManimon, S. K. & Casey, Z. A. (2018). (Re)Beginning and becoming with White practicing teachers: Notes on an educational foundations and curricular approach to antiracism and professional development. *Teaching Education, 29*(4), 395–406.

Tatum, B. D. (2017). *Why are all the Black kids sitting together in the cafeteria?: And other conversations about race*. Basic Books.

Thandeka. (2006). *Learning to be white money, race, and God in America*. Continuum.

Chapter 15 Discussion Questions

1. How does Casey challenge the traditional understanding of *praxis* in this chapter as simultaneous action and reflection? What are the practical and philosophical implications of reimagining praxis as a dialectical tension across time rather than a simultaneous activity?
2. Lather's (1991) concept of *catalytic validity* emphasizes transforming research participants' self-understanding and self-determination. How can researchers ensure this transformation occurs while avoiding extractive or objectifying practices, particularly when working with historically marginalized populations?
3. Casey critiques research that merely documents oppression without fostering humanizing change. How can qualitative researchers design studies that move beyond cataloging injustice to actively disrupting systems of oppression?
4. Casey highlights the importance of researcher reflexivity and positionality in qualitative research. How can researchers navigate the tension between their own identities and experiences and the needs and agency of participants, especially in studies aiming for transformative outcomes?

Biographies

Editor—Michael L. Boucher, Jr.

Texas A&M University-San Antonio

Michael Boucher is an Associate Professor of Curriculum and Instruction at Texas A&M University-San Antonio. Michael studies the interplay of race, power, and curriculum through his varied research examining the relationships of solidarity developed between successful white teachers and their students of color in de-facto segregated schools. His methodological work empowers individuals and communities to be co-participants in ethnographic education research. His 2020 book, *More Than an Ally: A Caring Solidarity Framework for White Teachers of African American Students*, articulates Caring Solidarity is a descriptive and aspirational framework for white teachers.

Robin Brandehoff

University of Colorado Denver

Robin Brandehoff is an Assistant Professor of Educational Foundations and oversees the Justice, Equity, and Diverse Identities Ed.D. program in the School of Education and Human Development at the University of Colorado, Denver. Her work and scholarship explore pedagogies of joy through critical and culturally sustaining theories of practice. Specifically, she examines the impact of critical mentoring and teacher preparation in historically marginalized communities through Hānai Pedagogy (Brandehoff, 2023), using decolonized methodologies, Grow Your Own teacher programming models, and community storytelling to collaborate with and educate at-promise youth, families, and the radical educators who journey in wonder with them.

Anglesia Brown

Wayne State University

Anglesia Lashaun Brown earned her Ph.D. in Educational Leadership and Policy Studies from Wayne State University. As a critical qualitative researcher, her work is rooted in Endarkened Feminisms and Black Feminist Thought, employing decolonizing methodologies to explore Black women's experiences in higher education. Her dissertation, *Triumphantly Taking Tenure: Reflections of Black Women Faculty in Higher Education*, examined the tenure journey of Black women faculty at predominantly white universities. In February 2024, she co-authored *Now You Get to See Me: Black Women Healthcare Professionals' Experiences in Sister Circles During the Double Pandemic*, in the *Journal of Qualitative Health Research*. She is co-editing the book *I Am Because We Are*, which highlights the transformative power of mentoring students of color. Dr. Brown holds two M.A. degrees, has extensive teaching experience, and is an active member of AERA and UCEA, where she is recognized as a Barbara Loomis Jackson Scholar.

Zachary A. Casey

Rhodes College

Zachary Casey is an Associate Professor of Educational Studies at Rhodes College in Memphis, TN, USA. His research and teaching focus on critical whiteness studies, teacher education, anticapitalism, and critical pedagogy. Focusing in particular on the ways neoliberal capitalism undermines antiracist praxis and pedagogies, his scholarship seeks to better understand the ways that white racial identities impact possibilities for a more humanizing education. Dr. Casey has published over 40 peer-reviewed journal articles, book chapters, and encyclopedia entries. He is the author or editor of several books focused on critical whiteness studies and critical pedagogy, including *A Pedagogy of Anticapitalist Antiracism*, and recipient of the Outstanding Book Award from the Society of Professors of Education. Routledge will publish his newest book, *Critical Pedagogy and the Trouble with Consciousness Raising*, in 2025.

Amy Castillo

Texas A&M University-San Antonio

Amy Castillo is an educational leader and academic coordinator for South San Antonio ISD and will soon finish her second master's in Curriculum and Instruction at Texas A&M University-San Antonio. She holds a bachelor's degree in interdisciplinary studies from the University of Texas-San Antonio and a master's in educational leadership from Stephen F. Austin State University. The focus of her master's thesis is *Resiliency in Spanish-speaking Latinos after Linguistic Oppression.*

DeShara C. Doub

Louisiana State University

DeShara Doub is a leader, public speaker, and mental health professional dedicated to social justice and advocating for marginalized communities. As the founder and CEO of Vision of Promise LLC, she empowers individuals by recognizing them as experts in their own lives. She holds a Bachelor of Science in Communication, a Master of Science in Social Work, and a certificate in Black Church Studies. She is pursuing a Ph.D. in Social Work, focusing on intergenerational trauma in historically Black institutions. As an ordained minister with certifications in Clinical Pastoral Education and Pre-Marital and Couples enrichment, DeShara has numerous honors, including a United States Special Congressional Recognition, Kentucky State Recognition, and the 2024 University of Louisville Emerging Leader award.

Miryam Espinosa-Dulanto

University of Texas-Rio Grande Valley

Miryam Espinosa-Dulanto is an Associate Professor at the Department of Bilingual & Literacy Studies, University of Texas-Rio Grande Valley. Miryam is an active scholar with a distinguished record of teaching, service, and professional activity. Her teaching and research draw on decolonial Indigenous feminist research methodologies. It is recognized by being transnational in scope yet intimately collaborative, using poetry, *testimonios*, *pláticas*, ethnography, and art-based qualitative methodologies. Miryam's scholarly and artistic publications appear in leading academic journals, handbooks, peer-reviewed books, and regional/local publications that evidence the broad interdisciplinary, community-based, and intellectual curiosity of her engagement.

Walter S. Gershon

Rowan University

Walter Gershon is an Associate Professor of Critical Foundations of Education at Rowan University. Dr. Gershon's scholarly interests focus on questions of justice and dignity about how people make sense, the sociocultural processes that inform their sensibilities, and the qualitative methodologies used to study the educational ecologies that render such understandings sensible. Drawing from critical social sciences, arts, humanities, and education, Walter's work often utilizes critical understandings in sound and the senses to consider everyday experiences of race, class, gender, and sexualities with disenfranchised children and youth. This combination creates opportunities for scholarly expressions that are sonically focused, as sounds embedded in text, texts that explicate sounds, and other possibilities that allow research collaborators and contexts to be heard without further mediation. Walter is also a working musician who plays Afro-Caribbean percussion and saxophones across genres and musical traditions.

Hope Hickerson

City of Baton Rouge, LA.

Hope Hickerson is the Executive Director of HealthyBR, Mayor Sharon Broom's Healthy City Initiative. With nearly two decades in the public health sector, Dr. Hickerson's career spans roles in university health centers, healthcare organizations, and public health initiatives. She holds undergraduate and graduate degrees in health education and promotion from East Carolina University, a master's in counseling, and a Ph.D. in Media & Public Affairs with a focus in health communication, both from Louisiana State University. Her research interests include understanding how messaging affects the well-being of marginalized communities, especially Black women.

Lorien S. Jordan

University of South Florida

Lorien Jordan is an Assistant Professor in Educational Measurement and Research (Qualitative Inquiry) at the University of South Florida. She is a critical qualitative methodologist who draws on critical theories of whiteness and colonialism, and experiments with creative, digital, and arts-based qualitative methods to interrogate and disrupt the cultural mechanisms of knowledge production. She has conducted this work in the United States, New Zealand, and Cambodia, and her work has been published in journals such as *Qualitative Research*, the *International Journal of Qualitative Methods*, the *International Review of Qualitative Research, and Cultural Studies ↔ Critical Methodologies.*

Tim Monreal

University of Buffalo

Tim Monreal is an Assistant Professor in the Department of Learning and Instruction at The University at Buffalo and is a 2024 Spencer Postdoctoral Fellow. His research broadly asks how (self) knowledge about Latinx is created and reproduced (in schools). More specifically, he is interested in the intersection of space/place on Latinx teacher identity and subjectivity and the teaching of Latinx history and content in social studies education. Tim increasingly uses (and develops) post-structural, post-humanist, and (relational) spatial theories and method(ologie)s to understand and nuance these concepts. He was previously a middle school (mostly social studies) teacher for 11 years. He was proudly born and raised in the Central Valley of California, is the eldest of nine brothers and sisters, and is now dad to three girls.

Geraldine Mooney Simmie

University of Limerick

Geraldine Mooney Simmie is a Professor of STEM Education and Director of EPI•STEM, The National Centre for STEM Education at the School of Education, University of Limerick, Ireland. Geraldine is an expert researcher with the European Commission on a new education study entitled *Social Transformations and Resilience Partnerships.* Geraldine retains a passion for education as a journey of becoming that involves commitment to one's ethical life project as well as learning to live well and actively participate with others in a search for the commons (democracy) in an ever-changing socio-cultural, affective, political, and material world. Geraldine's research interest is in teachers' work practices for human emancipation and, at the same time, for assuring the public interest values of a just and caring society and planet, (e.g., STEAM literacies). Geraldine's methodology specialism is in critical and feminist policy analysis. Find out more by listening to Geraldine's EPI•STEM Podcast.

Nabila Mushtarin

Louisiana State University

Nabila Mushtarin is a third-year Ph.D. student at the Manship School of Mass Communication, Louisiana State University. Originally from Bangladesh, she holds a Bachelor's and Master's in English and Cultural Studies from Jahangirnagar University and a master's in communication from the University of South Alabama. Her research interests include minority health, media effects, critical cultural studies, and social media dynamics, with a specific focus on marginalized and underrepresented groups.

Jasmin Patrón-Vargas

Texas A&M University

Jasmin Patrón-Vargas is an Assistant Professor at Texas A&M University. She received a dual doctorate from Michigan State University with a focus on Curriculum and Instruction and Chicano/Latino Studies. Her interdisciplinary scholarship attends to inquiries related to race, ethnicity, gender, and education. Her current research addresses the growing need to support schools and educators in implementing K–12 Ethnic Studies courses. She approaches this goal with two interrelated lines of inquiry: educational policy and pedagogy. Using critical policy perspectives, her first area of research explores the development of Ethnic Studies educational policies in the K–12 Social

Studies curriculum. Her second area of research draws on interdisciplinary perspectives in Teacher Education and Chicano/Latino Studies to examine the adoption of Ethnic Studies curriculum and instruction in secondary schools.

Nicole Roady

Chapman University

Nicole Roady's career and research in K–12 education have centered students and educators in their pursuit of educational freedom. As a former elementary teacher and current DEI practitioner, her passion for social justice work is interwoven throughout all aspects of her life. Nicole's scholarly interests include fostering dialogical spaces in education settings, critical pedagogy, diversity, equity, and inclusion initiatives in K–1 schools.

John H. Samuels

Mercer University

John "Hank" Samuels, an Assistant Professor of Elementary Education at Mercer University, works in teacher education. His research lies at the intersections of teacher education, professional development, creativity, and arts integration. He is specifically interested in examining how teacher educators, practicing teachers, and preservice teachers can cultivate joy and support the imagination-intellectual development of their students.

Shani Steyn

The IIE Varsity College, Cape Town

Shani Steyn is the Head of Education and Senior Lecturer at The IIE Varsity College Cape Town. Shani's research interests include transformative education, teacher empowerment, and issues such as the impact of imposter syndrome on first-generation South African students. She has presented her work internationally and authored *Currere from Apartheid to Inclusion: Building Culturally Responsive Pedagogies in Post-Apartheid South Africa*, where she advances culturally responsive pedagogies in post-apartheid contexts. Dr. Steyn contributes to the IIE Ethics Clearance Committee, serves on the editorial board of *Currere and Praxis*, and spearheads initiatives including inter-campus research symposia and a language center for non-native English speakers.

Christopher B. Tran

Chapman University

Christopher Tran's life, career, and body of work have revolved around his faith-oriented praxis and affinity for serving youth populations in situations of marginalization. Currently working as a school psychologist, Christopher supports students with various disabilities and mental health needs and students in alternative education settings. Beyond his profession, Christopher spends his free time volunteering in his community, specifically as a youth leader with his local church parish and diocese. Through the Catholic Restorative Justice and Detention Ministry, he is a volunteer in probation who serves youth impacted by incarceration. Recently graduating with his PhD in Education, Christopher's scholarly interests include examining Juvenile Justice, Critical Pedagogy, Liberation Theology, and Catholic Social Teaching.

Maranda C. Ward

The George Washington University

Maranda Ward is an Assistant Professor and Director of Equity in the Department of Clinical Research and Leadership in the GW School of Medicine and Health Sciences. She is an expert in advancing anti-racism efforts within health professions education and in designing curricula to enable students and faculty to competently promote health and racial equity in practice. Her research focuses on DEIJ and antiracism educational interventions as well as community-focused studies on HIV, Black women's health, and youth identity. She is also skilled in applying participatory action research (PAR). As affiliate faculty for the GW Honey W. Nashman Center for Civic Engagement and Public Service, she translated her PAR study on youth identity into a youth curriculum on preserving D.C. legacy. Maranda earned her Doctorate in Education from GW, her master's in public health from Tulane University, and her Bachelor's degrees in Sociology/Anthropology from Spelman College.

Asha S. Winfield

Louisiana State University

Asha Winfield is an Assistant Professor at Louisiana State University's Manship School of Mass Communication. As a critical/cultural media scholar, her research focuses on exploring the stories, rituals, and practices of Black individuals and communities as portrayed in media, culture, and society. As a multidisciplinary researcher, educator, and filmmaker, Dr. Winfield draws on intersectionality and Black feminist thought to foreground the lived experiences of Black people, examining how these experiences influence concepts such as audience reception, memory-making, and health behaviors. In 2022, she launched The Storytellers Lab at LSU, collaborating with students on arts-based research and documentary projects that spotlight underrepresented voices found particularly in the U.S. South. Her collaborative documentary, *Our Black COVID-19 Stories*, is scheduled for release by 2026.

Boni Wozolek

Penn State University-Abington

Boni Wozolek is the interim Associate Dean of Faculty Development for the Commonwealth Campuses of Penn State University. She is also an Associate Professor of Education for Penn State-Abington. Her scholarship focuses on qualitative research methods and teaching practices that attend to access, justice, and care for schools and student communities. Dr. Wozolek's book publications include two monographs—*Educational Necropolitics: A Sonic Ethnography of Everyday Racisms in U.S. Schools*, and *Assemblages of Violence in Education: Everyday Trajectories of Oppression*. She has also edited three volumes—*Black Lives Matter in US Schools: Race, Education, and Resistance; Queer Battle Fatigue: Education, Exhaustion, and Everyday Oppressions* (with David Lee Carlson); and *Letters to the Field: Curriculum Scholars' Stories for Future Generations* (with Walter S. Gershon and Roland Mitchell).

Index